## Where's Coase?

Ronald Coase's Nobel work outlined gains by reducing transaction costs and promoting property rights and markets to confront externalities. Countering market failure assertions and calls for centralized government intervention, Coase retorted that decentralized market negotiations could be welfare-improving by promoting collaborative, efficient problem-solving, and releasing resources to the general economy. Despite this, his approach is not central to any US environmental law implemented after 1970. Federal government mandates dominate. *Where's Coase?* explains why. The private objectives of political agents lead to policies that are likely to be too costly and inequitable, despite provision of public goods. Citizens face high collective action costs and lack information to distinguish between public goods and private agent benefits. Examining three major environmental laws, the Clean Air Act, the Magnuson–Stevens Fishery Act, and the Endangered Species Act, the book explores policy development and assesses the resulting costs relative to Coase's framework.

GARY D. LIBECAP is Distinguished Professor in the Bren School of Environmental Science and Management and Economics Department at the University of California, Santa Barbara, and Research Associate at the National Bureau of Economic Research. He was Pitt Professor in Economics at the University of Cambridge, 2010–2011, and Erskine Professor at the University of Canterbury (NZ), 2019. Libecap has long worked on the development and impact of property rights institutions, particularly for natural resources: oil and gas, timber, rangeland, minerals, water, and fisheries. He has authored or coauthored fourteen books and over 100 peer-reviewed articles and Libecap was awarded the Elinor Ostrom Lifetime Achievement Award in 2022.

RONALD COASE INSTITUTE SERIES ON NEW
INSTITUTIONAL ECONOMICS

The Ronald Coase Institute promotes research on the institutions – the laws, rules, customs, and norms – that govern real economies. This series summarizes key findings and provides new insights into how and why institutions matter for economic performance.

*Series editors*
**Alexandra Benham**
*Secretary to the Board, The Ronald Coase Institute*

**Lee Benham**
*Board Member, The Ronald Coase Institute, and Professor Emeritus of Economics, Washington University in St. Louis*

**Mary Shirley**
*President, The Ronald Coase Institute*

*Books in the series*

Why the Rush? An Institutional Economic Analysis of Homesteading and the Settlement of the West
*Douglas W. Allen and Bryan Leonard*

# Where's Coase?
## The Implications of Economic Property Rights or Rent-Seeking in Forming Institutions

GARY D. LIBECAP
*University of California, Santa Barbara*

Shaftesbury Road, Cambridge CB2 8EA, United Kingdom

One Liberty Plaza, 20th Floor, New York, NY 10006, USA

477 Williamstown Road, Port Melbourne, VIC 3207, Australia

314–321, 3rd Floor, Plot 3, Splendor Forum, Jasola District Centre, New Delhi – 110025, India

103 Penang Road, #05–06/07, Visioncrest Commercial, Singapore 238467

Cambridge University Press is part of Cambridge University Press & Assessment, a department of the University of Cambridge.

We share the University's mission to contribute to society through the pursuit of education, learning and research at the highest international levels of excellence.

www.cambridge.org
Information on this title: www.cambridge.org/9781009408073

DOI: 10.1017/9781009408080

© Gary D. Libecap 2026

This publication is in copyright. Subject to statutory exception and to the provisions of relevant collective licensing agreements, no reproduction of any part may take place without the written permission of Cambridge University Press & Assessment.

When citing this work, please include a reference to the DOI 10.1017/9781009408080

First published 2026

*A catalogue record for this publication is available from the British Library*

*A Cataloging-in-Publication data record for this book is available from the Library of Congress*

ISBN 978-1-009-40809-7 Hardback
ISBN 978-1-009-40807-3 Paperback

Cambridge University Press & Assessment has no responsibility for the persistence or accuracy of URLs for external or third-party internet websites referred to in this publication and does not guarantee that any content on such websites is, or will remain, accurate or appropriate.

For EU product safety concerns, contact us at Calle de José Abascal, 56, 1°, 28003 Madrid, Spain, or email eugpsr@cambridge.org

*To Ann*

# Contents

|  |  |  |
|---|---|---|
| List of Figures | | *page* xi |
| List of Tables | | xii |

1 The Implications of Economic Property Rights
  or Rent-Seeking in Forming Institutions  1
  1.1 Overview  1
  1.2 The Efficiency Case for Coase  9
  1.3 Framework: Economic Property Rights
      and Rent-Seeking  13
      *Economic Property Rights in Coasean Externality
      Mitigation*  13
      *Rent-Seeking in Externality Mitigation*  16
  1.4 Where Do We See Coasean Bargaining?  19
  1.5 Road Map  20

2 Economic Property Rights and Markets
  or Rent-Seeking: Arguments in the Institutional
  Economics Literature  23
  2.1 Overview  24
  2.2 An Institutional Revolution?  26
  2.3 A Brief Summary of the Institutional Economics
      Literature: Coase, Demsetz, and Economic
      Property Rights  29
      *The Institutional Economics Literature*  29
  2.4 Property Rights Contributions of Demsetz
      and Coase  32
  2.5 Timing of Institutional Scholarship  39
  2.6 Conclusion  42

3   Economic Property Rights: Adoption Worldwide
    and in US Environmental and Natural
    Resource Policy                                               45
    3.1  Introduction: Overview                                   45
    3.2  The General Empirical Record of Economic
         Property Rights                                          47
    3.3  US Environmental Laws                                    51
         *Overview: Where Is Coase? Why Is He Missing?*
         *What Has Been Lost?*                                    51
         *US Environmental Laws*                                  55
         *Institutional Frameworks for Collaborative*
         *Externality Mitigation*                                 57
         *Example of Prescriptive Regulation:*
         *The Clean Water Act*                                    58
    3.4  Conclusion                                               61

4   Transaction Cost Reduction or Rent-Seeking
    in Provision of a Public Good:
    The Clean Air Act                                             63
    4.1  Overview of the Clean Air Act: Decentralized
         Responses or Prescriptive National Regulation
         with Rent-Seeking in the Provision of a Public Good      64
    4.2  Legislative History of the Clean Air Act
         and the Adoption of Centralized Pollution Control        70
    4.3  Provisions of the 1963 Clean Air Act Amendments
         of 1970, 1977, 1990                                      77
    4.4  Costs of the Clean Air Act                               82
    4.5  Evidence of Rent-Seeking: Restricting Entry,
         Raising Rivals' Costs and Securing Particularistic,
         Strongly Held Goals via Clean Air Act Provisions         88
    4.6  Incentive-Based Instruments within
         the Clean Air Act                                        90
    4.7  Conclusion                                               92

5 Rent-Seeking, Economic Property Rights,
and Coasean Trade: US Fisheries Regulation    95
   5.1 Overfishing: Economic Property Rights and Coase
       versus Rent-Seeking and Prescription    96
   5.2 The Economic Problem: Economic and Biological
       Overfishing    102
   5.3 How to Address Open Access in Fisheries:
       The Theory    105
   5.4 Reaction to Open Access: Regulatory Controls
       and Limited Property Rights    108
       *Failure of Limited Entry Regulation*    *108*
       *Property Rights Constituency Positions*
       *and Political Limitations*    *113*
   5.5 Property Rights in US Fisheries    117
   5.6 Conclusion: Political Rent-Seeking and Constraints
       on Economic Property Rights and Markets    120

6 Rent-Seeking in Protecting At-Risk Species:
The Endangered Species Act (ESA)    124
   6.1 Introduction: Decentralized Coase or Centralized
       Prescription and Rent-Seeking in Species Preservation    125
       *Arguments in the Chapter*    *125*
       *A Decentralized Approach Not Taken*    *126*
       *Environmental Concerns and Adoption of Prescriptive*
       *Controls under the Endangered Species Act*    *133*
   6.2 The Endangered Species Act (ESA)    139
   6.3 Conclusion: Lessons of Rent-Seeking in the
       Endangered Species Act    151

7 What Have We Learned from the Absence of Coase?
Implications for the Formation of Institutions    154
   7.1 The Surprising Absence of Coase in Environmental
       Legislation    154

| | | |
|---|---|---|
| 7.2 | The Lessons of Coase | 157 |
| 7.3 | Rent-Seeking in Major Environmental Policies | 162 |
| 7.4 | Implications for Economic Property Rights and Rent-Seeking in Institutional Formation | 167 |
| Index | | 169 |

# Figures

| | | |
|---|---|---|
| 1.1 | Ronald H. Coase, Nobel photograph, December 1991. | *page 3* |
| 2.1 | Annual academic economics publications with property rights, transaction costs, or externalities in title. | 28 |
| 3.1 | World property rights extent and security. | 48 |
| 3.2 | World per capita GDP. | 49 |
| 3.3 | Global fisheries managed with property rights. | 50 |
| 3.4 | Cuyahoga River, Cleveland, Ohio, June 22, 1969. | 59 |
| 4.1 | Clean Air Act Uniform Ambient Air Quality Standards Non-attainment Counties. | 66 |
| 4.2 | Pittsburgh steel mill emissions, 1925. | 67 |
| 5.1 | Regional fishery management councils. | 101 |
| 5.2 | North Atlantic fish landings, 1935–1949. | 104 |
| 5.3 | Monterey sardine harvest, 1916–1967. | 104 |
| 6.1 | Critical habitat. | 132 |
| 6.2 | Annual Endangered Species Act (ESA) endangered or threatened listings, recoveries, extinctions. | 147 |
| 6.3 | Cumulative Endangered Species Act (ESA) listings, recoveries, extinctions, 1967–2024. | 147 |

# Tables

| | | |
|---|---|---|
| 2.1 | Selected academic work on economic property rights, markets, and performance. | *page* 30 |
| 5.1 | Constituency sentiments regarding catch shares property rights. | 114 |
| 5.2 | US fishery property rights. | 118 |
| 6.1 | Positions by interest groups on the 1995 reform and reauthorization of the Endangered Species Act (ESA). | 144 |

# 1 The Implications of Economic Property Rights or Rent-Seeking in Forming Institutions

> The problem is to avoid the more serious harm ... of choosing the appropriate social arrangement for dealing with the harmful effects. All solutions have costs and there is no reason to suppose that government is called for simply because the problem is not well handled by the market ... it is likely the extension of Government economic activity will often lead to this protection against the action for nuisance being pushed further than is desirable.

Ronald H. Coase, The problem of social cost.[1]

> [P]roperty rights develop to internalize externalities when the gains of internalization become larger than the cost of internalization.

Harold Demsetz, Toward a theory of property rights.[2]

> [S]ocieties choose different policies, some of which are disastrous for their citizens, because those decisions are made by politicians or politically powerful social groups that are interested in maximizing their own payoffs, not aggregate output or social welfare.

Daron Acemoglu, Why not a political Coase theorem?[3]

## 1.1 OVERVIEW

Coase or Pigou? Economic property rights and decentralized bargaining or centralized regulation and potential rent-seeking in the political arena in confronting externalities? That is the question for this volume.

---

[1] Coase, Ronald H. (1960). The problem of social cost. *Journal of Law and Economics*, 3 (October): 1–44.
[2] Demsetz, Harold. (1967). Toward a theory of property rights. *American Economic Review*, 57 (2): 347–359.
[3] Acemoglu, Daron. (2003). Why not a political Coase theorem? Social conflict, commitment, and politics. *Journal of Comparative Economics*, 31: 620–652, 621.

Pigou called on government taxes to equate marginal social benefits and costs for externality abatement.[4] Although such taxes are seldom used, Coase, as shown in Figure 1.1, framed his criticism of government intervention around Pigou's analysis. His efficiency-based alternative, however, also is seldom used. Prescriptive controls to address environmental externalities dominate. How those controls may facilitate costly rent-seeking in the political process and what that outcome means for broader institutional formation is the focus here.

Coase's 1960 "The problem of social cost" is among the most cited papers in economics and has stimulated extensive academic discussion.[5] This work and his 1937 path-breaking paper on firm organization were the bases for his 1991 Nobel Prize in Economics.[6] In 1960, Coase criticized standard prescriptive remedies for externalities as potentially excessively costly relative to the problem at hand. He offered a conceptual framework based on property rights and decentralized negotiation as a substitute.[7]

Despite their potential efficiency attractions, Coasean approaches are not central to *any* US environmental program as initially enacted. Command and control methods prevail. Incentive mechanisms sometimes are adopted late and in partial ways, especially in US fishery policies and aspects of the Clean Air Act.[8] The caps

---

[4] As described in the volume, Pigouvian externality controls rarely involve stylized taxes designed to equate marginal social and private costs. Instead, centralized regulatory controls are implemented ostensibly to impose costs on polluters as mitigation. An outline of Pigouvian approaches is provided in Salib, P. N. (2021). The Pigouvian constitution. *University of Chicago Law Review*, 88 (5): 1081–1156. See also discussion of Pigou and Coase in Hovencamp, H. (2009). The Coase theorem and Arthur Cecil Pigou. *Arizona Law Review*, 51: 633–649.

[5] Medema, S. G. (2020). The Coase theorem at sixty. *Journal of Economic Literature*, 58 (4): 1045–1128.

[6] Coase, R. H. (1937). The nature of the firm. *Economica*, 4 (16): 386–405; (1992). The institutional structure of production, University of Chicago Law School, *Occasional Paper*, 28.

[7] See Roumasset for formalizing key efficiency arguments in sharecropping contracts and their links to Coase. Roumasset, J. (1979). Sharecropping, production externalities, and the theory of contracts. *American Journal of Agricultural Economics*, 61 (4): 640–647.

[8] Aldy, J. E., Auffhammer, M., Cropper, M., Fraas, A., and Morgenstern, R. (2022). Looking back at 50 years of the Clean Air Act. *Journal of Economic Literature*, 60 (1): 179–232, 186.

FIGURE 1.1 Ronald H. Coase, Nobel photograph, December 1991.
*Source:* Nobel Foundation Archives, https://nobelprize.qbank.se/mb/?h=0f31241a156d13308f7cc6959804a8b2.
*Photo*: Boo Jonsson.

themselves are not negotiated by the using parties whereby costs and benefits would be weighed on a marginal basis in deciding upon controls. Further, allocation, durability, and exchange of use rights are restricted, and the rights explicitly are not a formal property right. These are, though, the necessary characteristics of a robust property rights regime. Observed arrangements are not the structures envisioned by Coase. They do not represent major shifts in mitigation efforts.[9]

While there has been plenty of time for his arguments to be incorporated in US policies, that has not occurred. The questions explored here are: Why not decentralized Coase? What are the possible efficiency, equity, and welfare outcomes of his absence? What might we learn from this exercise to better understand the motives for institutional development under different settings?

Is the lack of Coase's suggestions because the transaction costs are just too high? Are costs prohibitive for defining and enforcing property rights among polluters and pollutees and for their subsequent exchange? Is Coase just impractical? Do decentralized Coasean approaches encourage a competitive race to the bottom across regions? Do local citizens undervalue environmental assets of national concern? Would the assignment of property rights be too inequitable, dispossessing some, and encouraging degraded hot spots?

To address these questions, three US environmental policies are examined: the Clean Air Act Amendments of 1970, 1977, and 1990; the Magnuson-Stevens Fishery Act of 1976; and the Endangered Species Act (ESA) of 1973. The analysis draws upon legislative histories, law reviews, and relevant economics literature. Comparative

---

[9] See Keohane, N., Revesz, R., and Stavins, R. (1998). The choice of regulatory instruments in environmental policy. *Harvard Environmental Law Review*, 22: 313–367, 319-362 for discussion of rent-seeking and how it limited use of incentive-based instruments, including taxes, within prescriptive environmental regulation. If quantities of the externality were defined among decentralized parties (the cap) and tradable, the approach could be consistent with Coase. See Weitzman, M. (1974). Prices vs. quantities. *Review of Economic Studies*, 41 (4): 477–491. Libecap, G. D. (2025). State regulation of open-access, common-pool resources. In Ménard, C., and Shirley, M. M. (eds.). *Advanced Introduction to New Institutional Economics*. Edward Elgar Publishing, 545–572. He argues that fisheries were more organized at the local level to affect regulatory policies than in the case of other environmental legislation. They, however, were also heterogeneous with parties opting for rent-seeking to secure favored, non-tradable rights endowments.

empirical tests of alternative options across these three laws are not possible because centralized controls are ubiquitous, and we do not observe alternatives whereby property rights are assigned and traded in both setting and administering the cap. Accordingly, actual practices are compared with hypothetical Coasean alternatives. Applying a decentralized Coasean lens to existing legislation provides a metric for assessing what might be lost, if prescriptive regulation is not the low transaction cost, efficient, and more equitable option. It also suggests where Coase's decentralized approach might have been adopted but was not due to rent-seeking within the political arena.

With prescriptive regulation, the authority of the state is directed to set production, use, or emissions-release caps and to mandate compliance among regulated parties. The caps, individual constraints, and related costs and benefits are determined and allocated following negotiations among politicians, agency officials, and lobby groups. There generally is no direct role in the legislation for localized bargaining to equate marginal costs and benefits.[10] As political, not economic, distributions, regulatory controls inherently are inflexible and less responsive to new aggregate cost/benefit evidence.[11] Absent generally tradable property rights, there are no obvious market payment mechanisms to adjust behavior among polluters or pollutees, to redirect costs and benefits, or to better align incentives for compliance. Required behavioral, consumption, or production adjustments are enforced through imposed fines or related penalties for failure to observe regulations. Regulators, those regulated, and beneficiaries do not capture pecuniary *efficiency* gains. Polluters are motivated by the consequences of noncompliance and pollutees by private net gains delivered in environmental programs. In the absence of productivity motivations, the regulatory

---

[10] Again, with regional management councils, fisheries offer more opportunity for local bargaining, even though property rights were not implemented for twenty years in most fisheries.

[11] There is trade in aspects of the legislation – in fishery catch shares, in the Clean Air Act offsets, and in the $SO_2$ program.

constraints may be too extensive *or* too limited, depending upon lobby influence.

By contrast, under a property rights and decentralized exchange framework, these questions may be settled more effectively in a manner that reduces transaction costs. Where feasible, decentralized exchange may more optimally determine environmental controls and the distribution of costs and benefits involved. Resource use limits are negotiated by property rights holders, and exchange creates production constraints as externality mitigation with payments among the bargaining parties. Property rights could be assigned based on prior possession, the most dominant form of allocation. These issues and their impact on property rights are the thrust of the volume.[12]

Caps and allocations can be adjusted in response to new information through market trade. Negotiators are motivated by monetary gains from exchange to moderate externalities, considering shifting evidence of abatement costs and benefits. Negotiated outcomes are collaborative, with all parties having a stake in the process. Externality reduction is an asset to be exchanged and adjusted. The extent of abatement can be welfare-enhancing because tradeoffs are directly addressed in discussion between polluters and pollutees. In light of these attractions, the challenge is to explain why a Coasean framework was not implemented as the guiding structure of environmental laws.

The analysis presented in this volume outlines the efficiency arguments of Coase and compares them to actual policy operations.[13] Coase did not provide a blueprint for adoption. His work was part of the general conceptual literature on socially beneficial institutional change described in Chapter 2. Accordingly, the evaluation of

---

[12] Lueck, D. (1995). The rule of first possession and the design of the law. *Journal of Law and Economics*, 38 (2). Libecap, G. D. (1989). *Contracting for Property Rights*. Cambridge University Press, addresses distributional concerns in raising transaction costs. These issues and their impact on property rights are the thrust of the volume.

[13] Coase, The problem of social cost.

hypothetical Coasean exchange and actual environmental policies is not equally balanced. It is not one of apples to apples

As indicated in the legislative histories of US environmental policies, there is no record of a weighing of relative transaction costs by policy-makers of decentralized versus centralized approaches. Prescriptive controls do not appear to have been politically chosen because of their cost effectiveness. Why then are government-mandated restrictions imposed instead of more localized negotiated solutions in externality control? Can inferences be drawn for the efficiency of more general political responses in the economy, where property rights and markets might instead be chosen rather than government directives?

For externality mitigation, the answer presented in the volume is that rent-seeking in the political process by organized parties and their political and bureaucratic supporters has critically shaped observed regulatory patterns.[14] It displaces demand for economic property rights and use of markets. Rent-seeking can have a pejorative connotation, but that is not the purpose here. Rather, the concept is used positively to explain why and how parties use the political arena to achieve rents or benefits more extensively and at less cost compared to what they might have had to pay in a market. Moreover, these returns cannot be easily competed away. Overall, rent-seeking can result in inefficient resource allocation and use. It imposes higher aggregate costs and reduced net benefits relative to market outcomes, unless there are significant comparative transaction costs advantages with centralized regulation to alleviate externalities.

Rent-seeking is defined in the volume to include standard pecuniary or commercial returns to designated parties from preferential government policies that cannot be competed away. Rent-seeking is also defined more broadly than is standard to include philosophical values

---

[14] Tullock, G. (1967). The welfare costs of tariffs, monopolies, and theft. *Western Economic Journal*, 5: 224–232; Tullock, G. (2005). *The Rent Seeking Society*. Liberty Fund; Krueger, A. O. (1974). The political economy of the rent-seeking society. *American Economic Review*, 64 (3): 291–303.

granted by regulation to proponents at low direct cost. Private marginal benefits exceed private costs, and these nonpecuniary benefits or moral profits cannot be diminished by market entry and competition.

Especially in environmental regulation, rent-seeking provides value to some agents through strongly held, normative or philosophically driven objectives imposed by government on others. Advocates bear limited costs, often only lobby expenses. There may be public goods provided along with these personal gains, but the controls likely exceed levels where social marginal benefits and costs are equalized. Indeed, marginal benefit and cost calculations typically are not conducted in regulation, and agents have little incentive to do so. Further, rent-seeking takes place in the political assignment of preferential property rights that includes constraints on any subsequent trade in response to new cost and benefit information. The political objective of agents is to designate a relatively permanent allocation of ownership, production, and employment along with rents associated with it.

Rent-seeking in US environmental policies is associated with public goods provision, but the public goods may be more limited, costly, and controversial than they might have been had Coasean frameworks been central. Rent-seeking is successful because of differential collective action and information costs of externality mitigation between general citizens and more narrowly focused special interest groups, industry, or environmental nongovernmental organizations (NGOs).[15]

This explanation blends with the argument presented by Acemoglu.[16] He presents a framework and suggestive empirical evidence whereby members in societies are unable to contract to offset the losses imposed by self-interested parties because contractual remedies cannot be written and enforced over time. The transaction costs of doing so are prohibitive. Commitment problems are paramount.

---

[15] See Olson's law of large groups. Olson, M. (1965). *The Logic of Collective Action: Public Goods and the Theory of Groups*. Harvard University Press, 36.

[16] Acemoglu, Why not a political Coase theorem?

Proponents or opponents of environmental policies are apt to have lower collective action costs in the political arena than those in the general population. The former achieve policies that reflect their private objectives. Public goods may be provided. As a result, the general benefits delivered involve higher aggregate costs than would have been the case in a more openly negotiated Coasean framework. Under Coase, a fuller range of costs would be considered and weighed ex ante in adoption of environmental programs. Benefits would be more tailored to the interests of Coasean negotiators than to those active and proficient in the political process. Accordingly, citizens can be ineffective in moderating the effects of more partisan policies implemented through the efforts of better-organized groups, supportive politicians, and agency officials. Only if the aggregate costs become very high, might these collective action problems be overcome.

## 1.2  THE EFFICIENCY CASE FOR COASE

The quotations from Coase and Demsetz at the start of the chapter emphasize positive, optimistic institutional pathways to address economic issues previously associated in the 1950s with market failure. Their work was part of an emerging literature on the efficacy and welfare advantages of reducing transaction costs and achieving economic opportunities through property rights, markets, and related governance institutions.

In both his 1937 and 1960 papers, Coase outlined an efficiency argument for institutional and policy innovation. Agents adopted new institutions to economize on transaction costs and thereby making newly profitable exchange feasible. Resources could be reallocated; production redirected; and costs and benefits balanced. These motives are implicit in the 1960 article's parables of a farmer and livestock herder, railway and farmer, and confectioner and physician in describing the advantages of bargaining between polluters and pollutees to mitigate externalities.

Coase recognized that it was costly to devise and trade property rights, but he argued that it was not obvious that these transaction costs were higher than those associated with mandated caps and compliance enforcement. Coase claimed that costs were case dependent and that they ought to be compared in devising externality responses. The driving forces behind this approach were a better balance of net returns across the population, a more efficient level of externality control, and the release of more resources for use elsewhere in the economy. The agents involved were direct beneficiaries of these efficiencies, with broad social spinoffs.

As suggested by Coase, command and control regulations placed all abatement costs on polluters ("polluter pays"), giving them little stake in outcomes, with incentives to evade. It motivated pollutees to demand excessive regulation beyond where marginal social costs and benefits were equal, and for polluters to seek far less. With regulatory costs and benefits differentially distributed and lacking the straightforward trade of regulatory instruments for marginal adjustments of losses or benefits, a political battle for or against centralized controls would ensue. Unlike a market, there were no clearcut reasons for predicting that political exchange would lead to more efficient results and welfare improvements relative to the status quo.

Although Coase did not delve into the matter, government intervention for mitigation involved politics and the specific agendas of multiple interest groups, politicians, and agency officials. Even with the aim of providing broad public goods, there would be numerous interpretations of the externality problem and how to address it, each with different distributions of costs and benefits to the parties directly involved and to the general society. There would be both private and general benefits and costs, but self-interested political agents would be most concerned about and responsive to those costs and benefits they were most likely to bear. Narrow political interests would dominate. Agent objectives may or may not coincide with effective public goods provision.

Centralized regulation requires interest groups to raise alarms and to lobby politicians and agencies for action. Potentially regulated parties also would react to influence policies and reduce any regulatory costs placed upon them. The greater the range and complexity of externality, the more varied the disparate interests would be in promoting specific solutions, costs, and returns. Interest groups would lobby politicians and bureaucratic agencies for their desired policies. Unless there were multiple competitive interests in the political debate over externality control and the attendant release of information on mitigation costs and benefits to general citizens, politicians and bureaucratic agencies would be biased in favor of successful lobbyists. To the extent that marginal regulatory costs were not born by supporters, there would be an inherent push for constraints beyond those needed for efficient externality abatement.

By contrast, Coase argued that if polluters or pollutees held property rights, they could negotiate to mitigate production-imposed losses (or gains) in a decentralized manner. A more optimal externality level would result (generally not zero) with all parties having a tie to negotiated outcomes. It avoided the setting where Coase warned that costs could exceed benefits.[17] Negotiations required assignment and exchange of property rights, but Coase was agnostic as to whether they went to the polluter or pollutee.

In 1967, Demsetz augmented Coase's analysis by describing the development of property rights as economic (efficient) institutions and their essential role in market trade and promoting resource values. Together, Coase and Demsetz provided arguments for economic property rights and markets as efficiency-enhancing institutions. As new conditions or opportunities emerged, generating potential positive or negative externalities, parties would bargain for property rights adjustments and negotiate to internalize the externality. There were opportunity costs for not doing so and pecuniary gains (profits) from addressing the problem. The supply of property rights

---

[17] Coase, The problem of social cost, 39. As outlined in the legislative histories below, aggregate benefits may exceed aggregate costs for the Clean Air Act and Magnuson-Stevens Fishery Act, but marginal costs likely exceed marginal benefits so that overall, the regulations are excessive, at least in certain areas. For the Endangered Species Act (ESA), however, it is quite likely that total costs exceed total benefits.

and market solutions depended upon transaction costs that were real resource costs.[18] As with any costs, agents had incentives to innovate new institutional arrangements to lower transaction costs, engage in expanded trade, and achieve higher economic returns. These same efficiency objectives underlay the firm and market-level governance innovations outlined by Williamson.[19]

Because the benefits of economic property rights and markets seemed so profound, neither Coase nor Demsetz considered the rent-seeking opportunities afforded to some parties in the policy arena or how they might interfere with the emergence of efficient institutions. As argued earlier, rent-seeking reduces demand for economic property rights. Some parties could secure more private net returns through the political process and prescriptive controls than they could through the assignment of property rights and market exchange. These parties are motivated to organize politically to mold regulation along their desired lines and to achieve rents. Their actions, however, raise the transaction costs of mitigation by displacing property rights, market solutions, and their efficiency attributes. This potential challenge was not recognized by Coase or Demsetz.

Similarly, Williamson also did not explore the potential for rent-seeking to undermine the efficient governance responses he described. This threat, however, was far less problematic in his analyses because the private firm and market-level organizational

---

[18] Allen, D. W. (1991). What are transaction costs? *Research in Law and Economics*, 14: 1–18; Allen, D. W. (2000). Transaction costs. In Boudewijn Bouckaert and Gerrit De Geest (eds.). *Encyclopedia of Law and Economics, Volume I: The History and Methodology of Law and Economics*. Edward Elgar Publishing. Allen, D. W. (2012). *The Institutional Revolution: Measurement and the Economic Emergence of the Modern World*; Demsetz, H. (1968). The cost of transacting. *Quarterly Journal of Economics*, 82 (1): 33–53. Barzel, Y. (1982). Measurement cost and the organization of markets. *Journal of Law and Economics*, 25 (1): 27–48; (1989). *Economic Analysis of Property Rights*. Cambridge University Press.

[19] Williamson, O. E. (1975). *Markets and Hierarchies: Analysis and Antitrust Implications*. Macmillan Publishing; (1985). *The Economic Institutions of Capitalism: Firms, Markets, Relational Contracting*, Free Press; (1996). *The Mechanisms of Governance*. Oxford University Press; and (2010). Transaction cost economics: The natural progression. *American Economic Review*, 100: 673–690.

innovations of concern did not invite political entry, rent-seeking, and expensive institutional manipulation.

## 1.3 FRAMEWORK: ECONOMIC PROPERTY RIGHTS AND RENT-SEEKING

To frame the analysis of economic property rights, markets, externality control, and the competitive influence of rent-seeking, these concepts are now explored here in more detail. With this information, it will be possible to examine the absence of Coase in observed environmental regulation.

### Economic Property Rights in Coasean Externality Mitigation

Coase's approach for negotiated externality mitigation relies upon property rights and decentralized markets. Economic property rights define resource ownership, support trade, and allow for contractual innovation. They determine who has the recognized right to make decisions about asset use; devise organizational and contractual forms; engage in trade; and who captures the resulting net returns. Benefit maximization requires that property rights are exclusive, durable, and exchangeable.[20] Actual property rights are not ideal

---

[20] For discussion see, Barzel, Y. (1997). *Economic Analysis of Property Rights*. 2nd ed. Cambridge University Press, as well as Barzel, Y., and Allen, D. W. (2023). *Economic Analysis of Property Rights*. Cambridge University Press. The key attributes of economic property rights are outlined in Arnason, R. (2024). Individual transferable quotas in fisheries. In Shogren, J. F. (ed.). *Encyclopedia of Energy, Natural Resource, and Environmental Economics*. Elsevier Science; Arnason, R. (2012). Property rights in fisheries: How much can individual transferable quotas accomplish? *Review of Environmental Economics and Policy*, 6: 217–236; Runolfsson, B. (2024). Measuring quality of property rights: Development of user rights quality in the Icelandic Fisheries. *Marine Policy*, 160. February. There is debate over whether property rights are more usefully described as a bundle of sticks or more uniformly as modular institutions where attributes interact in influencing the impact of property rights on behavior. See Lee, B. A., and Smith, H. E. (2012). The nature of Coasean property. *International Review of Economics*, 59 (2): 145–155; Smith, H. E. (2025). The complex architecture of property rights, in Alston, L. J., Alston, E. C., and Mueller, B. (eds.). *Handbook on Institutions and Complexity: Emergent Institutions in a Complex World*. Edward Elgar Publishing; and Smith, H. E. (2024). Property law and economics. In Akkermans, B. (ed.), *A Research Agenda for Property Law*. Edward Elgar Publishing, chapter 5.

types. Their attributes vary due to transaction costs and related local assessments of fairness, openness, and morality.[21]

Demsetz described the development of property rights by agents as an economic institution in response to changing benefit/cost calculations.[22] His contractual adaptation to transaction costs is like Coase's and Williamson's for firm governance: Economic property rights are created or adapted "in response to the desires of the interacting persons for adjustment to new benefit-cost possibilities."[23] As with firm organization, property rights are dynamic institutions that vary in completeness and specificity across time and space according to the net returns from adjustment and transaction costs.[24] Agent efforts in defining and refining property rights not only advance individual welfare, but also generate broader economic well-being through market expansion and resource allocation to new economic activities. As noted above, observed property rights are not idealized institutions, but ones that are adjusted to actual conditions as second-best. Indeed, Demsetz cautioned against nirvana comparisons of transaction cost-free institutions with observed ones.[25]

In the firm level analysis of Coase and Williamson, economic property rights provide tradable rents or pecuniary returns to rights holders as defined and protected within the legal structure. They are implicitly held by agents in devising firm or market-level governance arrangements. Negotiating agents are residual claimants to the efficiencies afforded by institutional change to reduce transaction costs. An astounding array of efficiency-enhancing institutional innovations can be explained by this process. These include firm vertical integration; relational contracts; firm size, organizational hierarchies,

---

[21] Merrill, T. W., and Smith, H. E. (2007). The morality of property. *William and Mary Law Review*, 48: 1849; Wilson, B. J. (2020). *The Property Species: Mine, Yours, and the Human Mind*. Oxford University Press, 15.

[22] Demsetz, Toward a theory of property rights.

[23] Demsetz, Toward a theory of property rights, 350.

[24] Allen, What are transaction costs?; Allen, Transaction costs.

[25] Demsetz, H. (1969). Information and efficiency: Another viewpoint. *Journal of Law & Economics*, 12 (1): 1–22; Demsetz, H. (1988). The theory of the firm revisited. *Journal of Law, Economics, and Organization*, 4 (1): 141–161.

and boundaries; as well as team production arrangements; and use of boards of directors.²⁶ Critical insights have influenced scholarship, antitrust policies, and the auctioning of the spectrum.²⁷

Similarly, the potential monetary gains from cost savings and related efficiencies from the use of property rights and exchange are the bases for Coase's negotiated alternative to mandated constraints. Even so, in Coase's policy arena,²⁸ the efficiency motives of political agents and related broad welfare outcomes are far less straightforward than in his firm-level analysis of private actors.²⁹ Politicians,

---

[26] Coase, The nature of the firm; Coase, R. H. (1992). The institutional structure of production, University of Chicago Law School, *Occasional Paper*, 28. Williamson, *Markets and Hierarchies*; *The Economic Institutions of Capitalism*; *The Mechanisms of Governance*; and Williamson, Transaction cost economics.

[27] The literature is enormous. See, for example, Williamson, O. E. (1991). Comparative economic organization: The analysis of discrete structural alternatives. *Administrative Science Quarterly*, 36 (2): 269–296; Blair, M. M., and Stout, L. A. (1999). A team production theory of corporate law. *Virginia Law Review*, 85 (2): 247–328; Armour, H. O., and Teece, D. J. (1978). Organizational structure and economic performance: A test of the multidivisional hypothesis. *Bell Journal of Economics*, 9 (1): 106–122; Teece, D. J. (1981). Internal organization and economic performance: An empirical analysis of the profitability of principal firms. *Journal of Industrial Economics*, 30 (2): 173–199; Williamson, O. E. (1988). Corporate finance and corporate governance. *Journal of Finance*, 43 (3): 567–591; Masten, S. (1984). The organization of production: Evidence from the aerospace industry. *Journal of Law and Economics*, 27 (2): 403–417; de Figueiredo, J. M., and Teece, D. J. (1996). Mitigating procurement hazards in the context of innovation. *Industrial and Corporate Change*, 5 (2): 537–559. Spiller, P. T. (2009). An institutional theory of public contracts: Regulatory implications, in Menard, C., and Ghertman, M. (eds.). *Regulation, Deregulation, Reregulation – Institutional Perspectives*. Edward Elgar Publishing, 45–66, and Argyres, N., Mahoney, J., and Nickerson, J. (2019). Comparative adjustment costs and strategic responses to shocks. *Strategic Management Journal*, 40 (3): 357–376; Tirole, J. (1986). Hierarchies and bureaucracies: On the role of collusion in organizations. *Journal of Law, Economics, and Organization*, 2 (2): 181–214. Ménard, C., and Shirley, M. M. (eds.). (2005, 2008). *Handbook of New Institutional Economics*. Springer; (2022). *Advanced Introduction to New Institutional Economics*. Edward Elgar Publishing. Open access. www.elgaronline.com/monobook-oa/book/9781789904499/9781789904499.xml. Shapiro, C., and Shelanski, H. (2021). Judicial response to the 2010 horizontal merger guidelines. *Review of Industrial Organization*, 58: 51–79; Sullivan, E. T., Hovenkamp, H., Shelanski, H., and Leslie, C. R. (2019). *Antitrust Law, Policy, and Procedure: Cases, Materials, Problems*. Carolina Academic Press. For the spectrum, see Coase, R. H. (2013). The Federal Communications Commission. *Journal of Law and Economics*, 56 (4): 879–915.

[28] Coase, The problem of social cost.

[29] Coase, The nature of the firm.

agency officials, and members of lobby groups, who devise centralized controls, are not obviously motivated to economize on transaction costs in the same manner as in the private sector. They typically are not legally the direct recipients of the net returns of greater efficiencies. Rather, there is more opportunity for political rent-seeking via government intervention on behalf of specific, influential interests. Political assignment of the net returns from regulation involves partisan distribution of resource values, not the efficiencies of providing them.

*Rent-Seeking in Externality Mitigation*

A dynamic political rent-seeking framework is outlined by Keohane, Revesz, and Stavins, within the context of the Clean Air Act to explore why observed prescriptive policies rely so little on market or incentive-based instruments.[30] They do not explicitly examine why environmental policies are centralized in federal regulatory controls in the first place. They describe the demand for and supply of specific regulations across firms, individuals, unions, environmental interest groups, and legislators. They also do not explore an independent role for administrative agencies.

Merrill uses a similar rent-seeking approach to address the dominance of command and control and the limited use of incentive systems within them. He also explores why grandfathered permits rather than taxes are used whenever incentive instruments are adopted.[31] His explanation focuses on the tradeoffs among political agents in weighing wealth maximization versus distributional objectives in regulatory design.

Given command and control, Keohane, Revesz, and Stavins provide rent-seeking explanations for elements of the Clean Air Act, including more stringent regulation of new sources of pollution, than

---

[30] Keohane et al., The choice of regulatory instruments in environmental policy, 319–362.
[31] Merrill, T. W. (2000). Explaining market mechanisms. *University of Illinois Law Review*, 2000 (1): 275–298.

of existing ones, the sparce use of market instruments within prescriptive controls, the adoption of tradable permits not emission taxes, and the free allocation via grandfathering of those permits rather than auction.[32] Their equilibrium model illustrates the interaction among the agents demanding and supplying environmental policies.

Predictions of a rent-seeking framework include: (a) decentralized Coasean approaches for setting caps, and distributing property rights within it will be absent in policy; (b) the rare use of incentives within prescriptive policies; (c) the support of firms for grandfathered permits rather than taxes; (d) the limitation of the tradability of permits in order to restrict entry and production reallocation; (e) that firms, labor unions, and political supporters will seek to inhibit access, raise competitor costs, and constrain nonunionized operations; and (f) environmental NGOs will oppose markets on philosophical and strategic grounds. Prescription provides certainty of a fixed level of mitigation rather than one adjustable through exchange. (g) Politicians will prefer prescription because it advertises a specific level of environmental quality, and costs may be more hidden than under more transparent market trading.

Lobby groups bear narrow lobbying costs in promoting favored policies, while regulated parties and the general citizenry bear broader programmatic costs. Competitive interest groups, favoring different approaches to externality mitigation, can expose excessive costs or the granting of narrow benefits as rents to specific parties. The potential for such information to be released to general citizens cautions or constrains politicians and agency officials from going too far at the behest of special interests. Although there may be generalized benefits to citizens, the adopted approaches may not be the low cost or general welfare-improving ones.[33]

---

[32] Keohane et al., The choice of regulatory instruments in environmental policy, 314–317.

[33] Sallee, J. M. (2019). Pigou creates losers: On the implausibility of achieving pareto improvements from efficiency-enhancing policies. *NBER Working Paper*, No. 25831. May. National Bureau of Economic Research.

It is possible that difficulties in estimation might limit cost and benefit analyses in program design and implementation. Nevertheless, it is difficult to see why aggregate ex ante cost and benefit analyses as well as examination of their distributions, along with resulting ex post reassessments, would not be the first order of business for efficient responses to externalities. This is not the case empirically. Proponents have little interest in advertising costs and instead, are motivated to present them as integral in providing public goods. Smaller, well-organized, and more homogeneous interests, such as environmental NGOs or producer interests and labor unions, can promote desired programmatic outcomes. In return, they can promise political and bureaucratic supporters electoral and financial support. Opponents can be presented as thwarting the public interest in behalf of narrow private agendas. When there are few organized advocacy groups with different objectives, rent-seeking is more extensive, costly, and secure across political cycles.[34]

As suggested, rent-seeking controls can be far more static, inflexible, and protective of influential hierarchies. Innovation patterns that are set to meet regulatory approval may neglect more broadly beneficial investments in other new processes or products. Moreover, once in place, the distribution of rents generates entrenched stakeholders, who resist any subsequent redistribution.[35]

---

[34] It is remarkable given the role of government in environmental regulation that a critical public choice literature appears to be so limited. Generally, see Peltzman, S. (1976). Toward a more general theory of regulation. *Journal of Law and Economics*, 19 (2): 211–240; Olson, *The Logic of Collective Action*; Stigler, G. J. (1971). The economic theory of regulation. *Bell Journal of Economics*, 5: 3–21; Buchanan, J. M., and Tullock, G. (1962). *The Calculus of Consent*. University of Michigan Press; Becker, G. (1983). A theory of competition among pressure groups for political influence. *Quarterly Journal of Economics*, 98 (3): 371–400; Laffont, J. J., and Tirole, J. (1991). The politics of government decision-making: A theory of regulatory capture. *Quarterly Journal of Economics*, 106 (4): 1089–1127 and Johnson, R. N., and Libecap, G. D. (2001). Information distortion and competitive remedies in government transfer programs: The case of Ethanol. *Economics of Governance*, 2: 101–134.

[35] The persistence of ethanol subsidies despite the absence of any environmental or national security benefits is a telling example. See Bielen, D. A., Newell, R. G., and Pizer, W. A. (2018). Who did the ethanol tax credit benefit? An event analysis of subsidy incidence. *Journal of Public Economics*, 161: 1–14.

Over time, congressional oversight and control of agency actions may become less effective. Remedial legislative actions become more costly.[36]

Coasean market approaches, by contrast, challenge political rents by requiring that they be paid for, devoting actual budget outlays, and advertising policy outcomes. Moreover, decentralized exchange reduces the role of political actors and bureaucratic officials. It is not apparent how they would be made whole. Politicians lose the ability to trade policies for votes, and agencies lose mandates, budgets, and employment. Lobby groups rely upon controls for their preferred policies and specialize in developing additional political links and influence. These human capital skills lose value with market approaches. In his study of resistance to property rights in fisheries, Hannesson commented that inefficiencies create their own constituencies.[37]

## 1.4 WHERE DO WE SEE COASEAN BARGAINING?

Coasean bargaining is observed in smaller-scale settings (Ellickson 1982, Edwards 2016, Mulligan 2023),[38] which would be consistent with a low transaction cost argument. There are pecuniary benefits to agents in negotiating agreements to avoid neighboring trespass, compliance with homeowners' association rules, securing environmental easements, protecting groundwater, or the purchase and set aside of local ecologically valuable terrain.

Bargaining is also observed to lower the compliance costs and to encourage efficiencies with existing command and control regulations. Negotiations typically do not involve setting up the cap, which

---

[36] McCubbins, M., Noll, R. G., and Weingast, B. R. (1989). Political control of agencies. *Virginia Law Review*, 75: 431–482.
[37] Hannesson, R. (2006). *The Privatization of the Oceans*. MIT Press. 173.
[38] Ellickson, R.C. (1982) Cities and homeowners associations, University of Pennsylvania Law Review 130: 1519; Edwards, E.C. (2016). What lies beneath? Aquifer heterogeneity and the economics of groundwater management. Journal of the Association of Environmental and Resource Economists 3 (2): 453-491; Mulligan, C.B. (2023) Beyond Pigou: externalities and civil society in the supply–demand framework. Public Choice. 196: 1–18.

is preset by federal regulation. Deryugina et al. provide examples of polluters purchasing nearby lands as offsets, payments by consumers and government agencies for ecosystem services, and land acquisitions by government bodies and environmental NGOs to guard the supply of drinking water. Costello and Kotchen examine Coasean exchange alongside centralized government restrictions to control externalities.[39] They argue that property rights of some type and related trade reduce the costs of quantity restrictions in providing public goods.[40]

## 1.5  ROAD MAP

The timing for and key arguments of the literature on economic institutions and outcomes is summarized in Chapter 2. A brief overview of the contributions of Coase and Demsetz is provided. Chapter 3 confronts the theory with empirical evidence on a general absence of economic property rights and markets worldwide and more specifically, in US environmental and natural resource policies. In such policies, the lessons of Coase and Demsetz ought to be observed, but they are not.

For more microanalysis, Chapter 4 presents the legislative history and costs of the Clean Air Act. The Clean Air Act's health benefits are commonly emphasized, but there seemingly is less analysis in the literature of costs and tradeoffs and inequities imposed. Chapter 5 provides US fishery policies under the Magnuson-Stevens Act and the slow and abbreviated adoption of economic property rights, the most apparent solutions to open access. Input/output controls prevailed for the first twenty years of US fishery policy, despite

---

[39] Deryugina, T., Moore, F., and Tol, R. S. J. (2021). Environmental applications of the Coase theorem. *Environmental Science and Policy*, 120: 81–88; Costello, C., and Kotchen, M. (2022). Policy instrument choice with Coasean provision of public goods. *Journal of the Association of Environmental and Resource Economists*, 9 (5): 947–980.

[40] Costello and Kotchen examine the relative costs and benefits of tax (price) versus prescriptive controls (quantity) in instrument selection. See Weitzman who explored the conditions under which prices or quantity instruments would be the optimal policy mechanism. A quantity instrument maintains a fixed quantity of emissions for example, while potentially allowing the price of emissions permits to vary, whereas a price instrument maintains a constant price of emissions (tax) while allowing the quantity of emissions to vary. Weitzman, Prices vs. quantities.

evidence of over capitalization and excess harvests in regulated, open-access fisheries. Providing and protecting politically desired property rights to specific groups, along with controlling overfishing, created complicated and measured responses in US fishery externality regulation.

Chapter 6 turns to the poster child of US environmental regulation, the Endangered Species Act (ESA). The law is dominantly prescriptive and is molded by rent-seeking. ESA benefits in terms of actual species recovery appear to be surprisingly small, while its localized costs are high. Even so, it generates ardent support from key political constituencies, who secure at least philosophical rents. The ESA is politically contentious and is opposed by landowners who bear focused costs. These conditions likely explain the law's relative inflexibility and apparently limited outcomes. It illustrates Coase's warning that the structure of externality regulation could result in costs that exceed the problem at hand. Indeed, a Coasean approach likely would have been more biologically and economically successful. In fact, virtually all US environmental policies are stalled legislatively (although agency reinterpretations of existing laws remain active).[41] This is a puzzling outcome for legislation ostensibly aimed at providing public goods. It indicates the costs and their differential distributions across the population.

Chapter 7 provides a summary conclusion of economic property rights as defined in the literature and how their contributions are limited by nonmarket political goals, particularly with environmental policies. The legitimacy of nonpecuniary objectives is not questioned; rather it is argued that they might have been achieved more efficiently through the definition of and adherence to private economic property rights. But they were not. There are important observations. One is that economic property and markets have been

---

[41] EPA and other agency discretion has been constrained. Howe, Amy. (2024). Supreme Court strikes down Chevron, curtailing power of federal agencies. SCOTUS blog. June 28, 12:37 pm. https://shorturl.at/1WFFh.

restrained in policy choices, and it is likely that total social net benefits were reduced. A second is that local tradeoffs were not considered when centralized state policies were put into place. Accordingly, given political incentives and the distribution of costs and benefits that mold them, environmental policies may be too wide-ranging, too restraining, and too costly to advance total welfare on the margin. Finally, the implications of the absence of Coase in environmental laws, an area of specific focus in his 1960 paper, suggests that transaction cost efficiencies play a limited role in policy development. Although Coase offered an efficiency agenda for institutional formation rather than a blueprint for adoption, his decentralized suggestions have not been followed. Advocates seeking rents instead, have chosen centralized prescriptions.

# 2 Economic Property Rights and Markets or Rent-Seeking

*Arguments in the Institutional Economics Literature*

The rights of property, as such, have not been venerated by those master minds who have built up economic science; but the authority of the science has been wrongly assumed by some who have pushed the claims of vested rights to extreme and antisocial uses. It may be well therefore to note that the tendency of careful economic study is to base the rights of private property not on any abstract principle, but on the observation that in the past they have been inseparable from economic progress ...

Alfred Marshall, *Principles of Economics.*[1]

economists have misdirected their efforts ... in the search for the explanation of economic growth ... the answer lies in the characteristics of the basic institutional environment ... If those rules lower the costs and raise the benefits of institutional arrangements that redistribute income, relative to those that encourage (by profitable incentive) institutional arrangements which increase output, then that society will devote its energies accordingly.

D. C. North, Institutional change and economic growth.[2]

governance is the means by which to infuse order, thereby to mitigate conflict and realize mutual gain. Furthermore, the transaction is made the basic unit of analysis.

O. E. Williamson, Transaction cost economics.[3]

---

[1] Quoted in Scott, A. (1955). The fishery: The objectives of sole ownership. *Journal of Political Economy*, 63 (2): 116–124, 116: Alfred Marshall, *Principles of Economics* (1890) 8th ed.: 48.
[2] North, D. C. (1971). Institutional change and economic growth. *Journal of Economic History*, 31 (1): 124.
[3] Williamson, Transaction cost economics.

## 2.1 OVERVIEW

This chapter places Coase, Pigou, and the US environmental policies examined in this volume into the broader context of the literature on the economics of institutional change.[4] This academic research provides background for Coasean bargaining and suggests the tradeoffs that emerge when decentralized approaches to economic problems are displaced by those of centralized regulation. Relevant referenced studies cover economic property rights, transaction costs, institution formation, governance, contracting, and economic performance. The analyses point to significant economic and social welfare advantages when transaction costs are reduced and markets are advanced. The discussions fit squarely with Coase's more focused framework for addressing externalities in an efficient, beneficial manner.

As demonstrated in Chapter 3, however, the adoption of economic property rights and markets across a variety of world settings is more limited than their productive improvements would suggest. North et al., Acemoglu, and Acemoglu and Robinson use macro-level examples in the political arena to suggest why segments of populations worldwide might chose a less efficient route.[5] Similarly, as noted in Chapter 1, Coase's efficiency remedies to confront externalities also have not been the principal initial thrust of US environmental laws. The explanation offered here is that rent-seeking is a competitor for economic property rights and markets in the

---

[4] Coase, The problem of social cost; Pigou, A. C. (1920). *The Economics of Welfare*. Macmillan.

[5] Acemoglu, Why not a political Coase theorem?, 621; North, D. C., Wallis, John Joseph, and Weingast, Barry R. (2009). *Violence and Social Orders*. Cambridge University Press. Acemoglu, D. and Robinson, J. A. (2012). *Why Nations Fail*. Crown Business. See also, Johnson, S. (2024). Disease environments, the mortality of Europeans, and the creation of institutions in the colonial era. Nobel Lecture; Acemoglu, D. (2024). Institutions, technology and prosperity. Nobel Lecture; and Robinson, J. A. (2024). Paths towards the periphery. Nobel Lecture. Summary discussions of the three Nobel Prize winners, Dell, Melissa. (2024). Institutions and prosperity: The 2024 Nobel laureates. https://shorturl.at/aulPr.

environmental arena and also generally elsewhere in the economy.⁶ This is also the explanation offered by Keohane et al. for the rare, late, and limited adoption of incentive-based instruments in US environmental laws.⁷ As the above quotations by Marshall and North suggests, political rent-seeking and the inefficient institutions it supports can be extremely costly for societies.

Environmental policies may seem an unusual topic for exploring the formation of institutions and neglect of economic property rights. As we will see, there is no doubt that the environmental programs discussed in Chapters 3–6 have brought many improvements over the status quo. But that is precisely why attention to rent-seeking in environmental policies is so useful. Even where apparently advantageous policies have been implemented, they can still be distorted in socially costly ways, making them less beneficial on net. Despite the positive public good attributes of these policies, overall social costs are raised and programmatic characteristics distorted to advantage influential parties. Favorable public good offsets may not be found for example with some protective tariff policies or other rent-seeking interventions that might diminish economic performance. Understanding how rent-seeking in environmental policies takes place provides insights into how otherwise efficient institutional formation can be thwarted by self-interested parties in the political arena. It also helps to explain why the transaction cost literature associated with Coase, Williamson, and Demsetz has been far more influential in the private sector, where agents are the residual claimants of efficiencies and not politically based rents.⁸

The enactment of environmental programs illustrates the information and collective action challenges faced by general citizens

---

⁶ Tullock, The welfare costs of tariffs, monopolies, and theft; *The Rent-Seeking Society*; Krueger, The political economy of the rent-seeking society.
⁷ Keohane et al., The choice of regulatory instruments. Merrill, Explaining market mechanisms, also points to rent-seeking along with distributional conflicts in molding property rights and markets.
⁸ Williamson, Transaction cost economics; Coase, The problem of social cost, 44; and Demsetz, Toward a theory of property rights.

when policies are put into place with a combination of private rent-seeking and public goods objectives. Citizens must separate general from particularistic benefits to ensure policies are as socially beneficial as possible.[9] In doing so, however, they confront the efforts of well-organized special interests with narrow rent-seeking aims. By contrast, the citizenry is more heterogeneous and larger with multiple interests and concerns, which makes it difficult to mobilize reaction against more focused groups. Moreover, citizens often lack information on actual costs and benefits. As noted in Chapter 1, only when costs become too high to be hidden or ignored, might citizens' collective action problems be circumvented. By that time, however, serious, potentially path-dependent costs may be inflicted.

This chapter explores the process of institutional formation and how it can be directed inefficiently. It begins by outlining the benefits of economic property rights and Coase's framework, drawing from the institutional economics literature. Much of the relevant academic work appeared in the latter half of the twentieth and early part of the twenty-first centuries, and this timing is explored. Although not explicit in the literature, the transaction cost literature appears to have been in reaction to standard, Keynesian market failure arguments of the post-World War II period. These market failure arguments neglected transaction costs and the motives of private agents to economize on them. Indeed, Coase's property rights and market approach was an explicit challenge to market failure claims and their associated government remedies.[10]

## 2.2 AN INSTITUTIONAL REVOLUTION?

The quotations above by Alfred Marshall, Douglass North, and Oliver Williamson emphasize the essential role of property rights

---

[9] Volden, C., and Wiseman, A. E. (2007). Bargaining in legislatures over particularistic and collective goods. *American Political Science Review*, 101 (1): 79–92.

[10] Externalities arise from the absence of complete property rights. See Cheung, N. S. (1970). The structure of a contract and the theory of a non-exclusive resource. *Journal of Law and Economics*, 13 (1): 49–70.

and governance institutions in promoting economic outcomes that advance social welfare. Institutions, both those favorable and those damaging to efficiency, are endogenous within societies as both theory and research have shown. In the preface to *Advanced Introduction to New Institutional Economics*, Claude Ménard and Mary Shirley summarize core advantages of research on institutions and suggest its influence on economics, political science, management, law, and sociology. They emphasize Coase's expectation that a vibrant research agenda would not only transform economics, but also intellectual and policy debates.[11]

Ménard and Shirley are prescient in many ways. New understanding has been articulated about governance institutions in organizations and markets, as well as the role of economic property rights in setting the institutional bases for economic growth. The literature surveyed here emphasizes the critical role of private agents in reducing transaction costs because they capture the net gains from doing so. These parties are the engines of efficiency-enhancing institutional change. The process results in more effective and profitable organizational forms, firms, and market expansion. They can advance secure, transferable property rights to curb externalities, reduce open-access losses, promote long-term investment, encourage innovation, and redeploy assets to more profitable uses.

The leaders in this literature were awarded Nobel Prizes in Economic Science for their contributions: Ronald H. Coase (1991), Douglass C. North (1993), Oliver E. Williamson (2009), Elinor Ostrom (2009), Daron Acemoglu, James A. Robinson, and Simon H. Johnson (2024).[12] An active research society, the Society for Institutional and Organizational Economics (formerly the International Society for

---

[11] Ménard and Shirley (eds.), *Advanced Introduction to New Institutional Economics*, x. Coase, R. H. (1998). The new institutional economics. *American Economic Review*, 88 (2): 72–74.

[12] Acemoglu, Institutions, technology and prosperity; Robinson, Paths towards the periphery; Johnson, Disease environments.

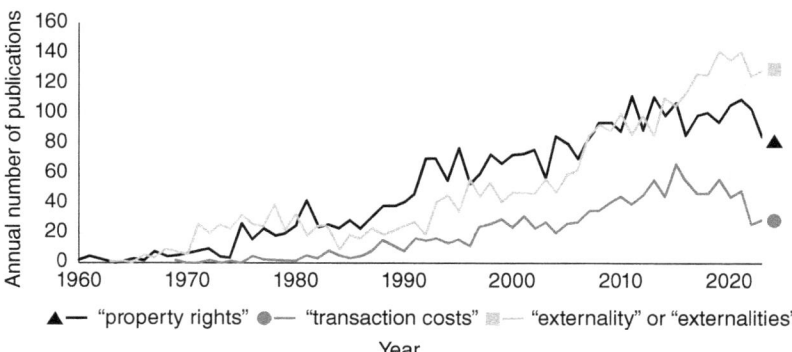

FIGURE 2.1 Annual academic economics publications with property rights, transaction costs, or externalities in title.
Source: Calculated from data in Web of Science – Social Science Citation Index. https://en.wikipedia.org/wiki/Social_Sciences_Citation_Index.

New Institutional Economics) was founded in 1996. The society meets annually and has a membership of approximately 150 researchers.

Figure 2.1 depicts the number of academic economics articles published annually with property rights, transaction costs or externalities in the title between 1960 through 2023. Publications addressing all three topics rose after Coase's article in 1960, revealing a profound rise in interest in economic institutions for over fifty years.

Despite this large and growing literature, the actual role played by property rights and markets in environmental policy appears far more limited than Coase's 1998 prediction, notwithstanding the advances in firm governance and organizations associated with Williamson. Indeed, the outcomes fit more generally with more pessimistic conclusions in broader empirical studies by Acemoglu, North et al., and Acemoglu and Robinson.[13]

---

[13] Williamson, *Markets and Hierarchies*; *The Economic Institutions of Capitalism*; *The Mechanisms of Governance*; and Transaction cost economics; Acemoglu, Why not a political Coase theorem?, 621; North et al., *Violence and Social Orders*; Acemoglu and Robinson, *Why Nations Fail*.

## 2.3 A BRIEF SUMMARY OF THE INSTITUTIONAL ECONOMICS LITERATURE: COASE, DEMSETZ, AND ECONOMIC PROPERTY RIGHTS

### The Institutional Economics Literature

A complete literature review is not attempted here on the roles of institutions, governance, and contracting as a means of reducing transaction costs and advancing efficient economic organization and performance. The most complete summary is provided by Ménard and Shirley.[14] Nevertheless, some contributions are emphasized for key points as background for assessing Coase's externality mitigation framework.

Table 2.1 lists academic analyses of economic property rights and markets. Not included is the very rich and extensive literature on firm structures, organization, and contracts, referenced in Chapter 1. Entries are organized by those studies that described a theory of institutional formation with predicted outcomes; empirical analyses of the complexities encountered; the costs of inefficient arrangements; the transaction costs of organization structures and exchange; and political factors underlying the process of institutional change, of concern in this volume.

This listing from the literature, albeit incomplete, indicates just how remarkably far ranging it has been.[15] The academic work

---

[14] Ménard and Shirley (eds.), *Handbook of New Institutional Economics; Advanced Introduction to New Institutional Economics.*

[15] Other important work includes, Keefer, P., and Vlaicu, R. (2007). Democracy, credibility, and clientelism. *Journal of Law, Economics and Organization*, 24 (2): 371–406; Lueck, The rule of first possession; Klein, B., Crawford, R. G., and Alchian, A. A. (1978). Vertical integration, appropriable rents, and the competitive contracting process. *Journal of Law and Economics*, 21 (2): 297–326; La Porta, R., Lopez-de-Silanes, F., and Shleifer, A. (2008). The economic consequences of legal origins. *Journal of Economic Literature*, 46 (2): 285–332. Ellickson, R. C. (1993). Property in land. *Yale Law Journal*, 102: 1315–1397. Sallee, Pigou creates losers; Smith, H. E. (2012). Property as the law of things. *Harvard Law Review*, 125: 1691–1726; and Edwards, E. C., Fiszbein, M., and Libecap, G. D. (2022). Property rights to land and agricultural organization: An Argentina–United States comparison. *Journal of Law and Economics*, 65 (S1): 1–33.

Table 2.1 Selected academic work on economic property rights, markets, and performance

| Development of economic property rights and predicted outcomes | Empirical analyses of institutional formation and economic performance | Transaction costs in institutional organization and exchange | Political and legal factors in institutional formation |
|---|---|---|---|
| Coase (1937, 1960) | North and Thomas (1973) | Coase (1937, 1960) | Buchanan and Tullock (1962) |
| Gordon (1954) | Libecap (1978, 1989) | Cheung (1970) | Olson (1965) |
| Scott (1955) | North (1981, 1990) | Williamson (1975, 1985, 1996) | Stigler (1971) |
| Demsetz (1964, 1967, 1969) | Johnson and Libecap (1982) | Barzel (1982, 1989) | Posner (1973) |
| Ostrom (1990) | Libecap and Wiggins (1984, 1985) | Allen (2000) | Peltzman (1976) |
|  | Wiggins and Libecap (1985) |  | Laffont and Tirole (1991) |
|  | Acemoglu et al. (2001, 2002) |  |  |
|  | Acemoglu and Johnson (2005) |  |  |
|  | Acemoglu and Robinson (2012) |  |  |
|  | North et al. (2009) |  |  |

Sources:

Demsetz, H. (1964). The exchange and enforcement of property rights. *Journal of Law and Economics*, 7: 11–16; Toward a theory of property rights; Information and efficiency.

North, D. C. (1981). *Structure and Change in Economic History*. W. W. Norton; (1990). *Institutions, Institutional Change, and Economic Performance*. North, D. C., and Thomas, R. P. (1973). *The Rise of the Western World: A New Economic History*. North et al., *Violence and Social Orders*.

Acemoglu, D., and Johnson, S. (2005). Unbundling institutions. *Journal of Political Economy*, 113 (5): 949–995;

Acemoglu and Robinson, *Why Nations Fail*; Acemoglu, D., Johnson, S., and Robinson, J. (2001). Colonial origins of comparative development: An empirical investigation. *American Economic Review*, 95 (1): 1369–1401; (2002). Reversal of fortune: Geography and institutions in the making of the modern world income distribution. *Quarterly Journal of Economics*, 117 (4): 1231–1294.

Allen, Transaction costs.

Cheung, The structure of a contract.

Posner, R. A. (1973). *Economic Analysis of Law*.

Libecap, G. D. (1978). Economic variables and the development of the law: The case of western mineral rights. *Journal of Economic History*; Contracting for Property Rights; (1982) with Johnson, R. N. Contracting problems and regulation: The case of the fishery. *American Economic Review*; (1984) with Wiggins, S. N. Contractual responses to the common pool: Prorationing of crude oil production. *American Economic Review*; (1985) with Wiggins, S. N. The Influence of private contractual failure on regulation: The case of oil field unitization. *Journal of Political Economy*; (1985) with Wiggins, S. N. Oil field unitization: Contractual failure in the presence of imperfect information. *American Economic Review*, 75 (3): 368–385.

Barzel, Y. (1982). Measurement costs and the organization of markets. *Journal of Law and Economics*, 25 (2): 27-48; (1989). *Economic Analysis of Property Rights*.

Williamson, O. E. (1975). *Markets and Hierarchies: Analysis and Antitrust Implications*; (1985). *The Economic Institutions of Capitalism: Firms, Markets, Relational Contracting*; *The Mechanisms of Governance*.

Ostrom, E. (1990). *Governing the Commons: The Evolution of Institutions for Collective Action*.

Olson, *The Logic of Collective Action*.

Buchanan and Tullock, *The Calculus of Consent*.

Laffont and Tirole, The politics of government decision-making.

Stigler, The economic theory of regulation.

addresses the opportunities for institutional responses to fundamental economic problems by lowering transaction costs along with empirical records of accomplishment or underperformance.

North's work gives a clear sense of how property rights institutions and markets determine economic consequences. North defined institutions as "humanly devised constraints that structure political, economic and social interactions."[16] Later North described: "Modern economic growth results from the development of institutions that permit an economy to realize the gains from specialization and division of labor ..." Institutions influence the array of benefits and costs available to individuals in economic decision-making for investment, production, and trade. Accordingly, the institutional structure of the society defines the incentives for productive activities, the mechanisms by which contacts are written and enforced, time horizons, and the distribution of the net returns of economic activity. North concluded, however: "In fact, one of the most evident lessons from history is that political systems have an inherent tendency to produce inefficient property rights which result in stagnation or decline."[17]

Despite North's pessimistic observation about political intervention in the economy, Coase and Demsetz define more optimistically how economic property rights in private settings can support markets, promote efficient economic behavior, and generate improved economic performance.

## 2.4 PROPERTY RIGHTS CONTRIBUTIONS OF DEMSETZ AND COASE

Arguably the most important contributions for understanding institutional development and the potential of economic property rights are those by Demsetz and Coase. Their academic arguments became the bases for a large and provocative literature on when and how

---

[16] North, *Structure and Change in Economic History*, 36.
[17] North, D. C. (1987). Institutions, transaction costs, and economic growth. *Economic Inquiry*, 25 (3): 419–428 at 422.

property rights emerge as economic institutions, and their potential role in molding beneficial economic decisions and in mitigating externalities. Jointly, their work challenged traditional centralized regulation that was based upon market failure assertions. As noted in Chapter 1, Coase and Demsetz were skeptical of the efficacy of centralized prescriptive approaches, even with public goods claims as justification, and pointed to the transaction costs and misaligned incentives encountered. They argued that there was no ideal regulatory reaction to externalities. Demsetz cautioned that it was inappropriate to compare market failure with perfect government regulation, just as it was inappropriate to compare government failure with a perfect market. Responses by both would be incomplete and costly. Coase called for comparisons of institutional performance and costs in any policy recommendation. Neither, however, examined the rent-seeking incentives and nonpecuniary aims that we will see have influenced actual environmental regulation.

Prior to the work of Demsetz in particular, economists generally had assumed the existence of property rights and markets. Where they were asserted to be incomplete, market failure was viewed as a rationale for government intervention via corrective taxes or regulation.[18] Economists had not seriously examined property rights as economic institutions that not only determined what would be included in market exchange, but also what would be efficiently left outside it. According to Coase and Demsetz, the presence of externalities was not necessarily evidence of market failure nor of need for government remedy.

In a remarkable series of almost annual papers. Demsetz gave structure for Coasean approaches and for markets in promoting efficiency and smoothing asset reallocation.[19] Markets required

---

[18] Pigou, *The Economics of Welfare*; Bator, F. M. (1958). The anatomy of market failure. *Quarterly Journal of Economics*, 72: 353–354, 358; Baumol, W. J. (1972). On taxation and the control of externalities. *American Economic Review*, 62 (3): 307–322.

[19] Demsetz, The exchange and enforcement of property rights; Toward a theory of property rights; The cost of transacting; Information and efficiency; The theory of the firm

property rights and traders, who were residual claimants to the profits earned by responding to shifts in costs and benefits. As such, property rights were the most fundamental economic institution in a society. They determined ownership and authority for economic decisions, their range and nature, the flow of economic returns and costs, and motives for exchange. The extent to which property rights were secure set timelines and determined the relative attraction of current consumption versus longer-term investments. Property rights also created opportunities and inducements for institutional innovation.

Demsetz asserted that property rights were economic institutions with benefits and costs, including the transaction costs in setting up, refining, enforcing, and trading rights. He provided a contractual theory of the supply and demand for property rights with profit-maximizing agents investing in them based upon expected net returns.

Demsetz illustrated this conjecture with the progression of property rights to land among the Montagnes peoples in seventeenth-century Quebec as chronicled by anthropologist Eleanor Leacock.[20] The rise of the fur trade and greater pressure on resident beaver populations drove up implicit land values as well as the costs of open-access trapping externalities that potentially could deplete beaver stocks. Over time, free trapping was replaced by private territorial privileges with seasonal hunting allotments. Individual hunting grounds were marked by visible tree blazes. Leacock found that by the middle of the century, allotted territories were relatively stable, seemingly displacing what had been unrestricted territorial entry. Although property rights to mobile beaver would entail high transaction costs, claims to stationary land that beaver inhabited could be defined and enforced at lower cost. The observed institutional

revisited; (1996). The core disagreement between Pigou, the profession, and Coase in the analyses of the externality question. *European Journal of Political Economy*, 12 (4): 565–579.

[20] Demsetz, Toward a theory of property rights, 351–352.

pattern was consistent with Demsetz's proposed rights progression. The focus was on the asset where rights could be implemented at least cost (land, not beaver). Demetz also used fisheries as an indication of the problem of open access that would be solved with property rights once there was enough value in fish to outweigh the cost of establishing property rights.[21]

As examined in Chapter 5, until modern times, most wild ocean fish stocks were so abundant relative to harvests that there was little return for investing in them. They were exploited as if stocks were unlimited, which for a while, they were. Potentially more valuable resources, by contrast, attracted more competition and generated more attention to establishing property rights. In the case of fisheries, by the last half of the twentieth century, as harvests rose dramatically with new technologies and rising demand for fish, populations dropped. The remaining fish became more valued and efforts to define property institutions took place where possible. Countries with coastal zones declared state ownership of waters within 200 miles of their shores and restricted entry by noncitizen fishers. They, however, did far less in assigning property rights among citizens to their newly claimed waters. Political imperatives intervened. As indicated in the following chapter, the process of defining property rights in world fisheries has been very incomplete, likely in large part because of interference from political rent-seeking within countries rather than transaction cost constraints.[22] Even so, the general pattern in fisheries corresponds with Demsetz's predictions and his Montagnes example.

---

[21] To more completely test Demsetz's hypothesis, Libecap, follows the rise in mineral land values along Nevada's Comstock Lode after 1859 due to new ore discoveries that in turn led claimants to seek to greater precision in the definition and enforcement of mining claims via private agreements, court rulings, and legislative actions. Libecap, Economic variables. See also, Libecap, G. D. (1986). Property rights in economic history: Implications for research. *Explorations in Economic History*, 23 (3): 227–252.

[22] For discussion of the challenges and costs in world fisheries, see World Bank, Food and Agriculture Organization, Arnason, R., Kelleher, K., and Willmann, R. (2009). *Sunken Billions: The Economic Justification for Fisheries Reform*. World Bank.

According to Demsetz, there was an efficient range of property rights completeness, depending on costs and benefits. Along this continuum, where the property right was less complete due to transaction costs, fewer attributes would be covered. Demsetz argued that observed markets and property rights at any point in time depended upon transaction costs, which would never be zero, and the potential value or profitability of modifying them. Not all externalities would be eliminated, nor would markets be complete in every dimension. Low-valued resources, for instance, that were difficult to observe or bound and were faced with minimal competition for control might have limited property rights.

Demsetz argued that transaction costs were real resource costs just like those associated with any productive input.[23] Economic agents had the same incentives for lowering them as they would have for other costs. Property rights modification and exchange were part of a welfare-maximizing, institutional formation process. In zero transaction cost settings, all valuable resource attributes would be owned and traded. There would be no third-party effects of consumption, production, or trade. Although Demsetz commented that "a community's preferences for private ownership" would play a role in the pattern of rights definition,[24] he did not explore the issue nor the ways in which political rent-seeking might affect how property rights might actually be defined, enforced, and traded.[25]

Coase used externality, a quintessential example emphasized by those who claimed market failure, to illustrate how economic property rights and markets could be a lower cost, efficient

---

[23] Demsetz, The cost of transacting; Barzel, Measurement cost and the organization of markets; Allen, Transaction costs. Merrill, Explaining market mechanisms, and Libecap, *Contracting for Property Rights* point to distributional conflicts in raising the transaction costs of property rights definition and exchange.

[24] Demsetz, Toward a theory of property rights, 350.

[25] For discussion of political factors, although not rent-seeking in particular, see Peltzman, Toward a more general theory of regulation. Olson, *The Logic of Collective Action*; Stigler, The economic theory of regulation. Buchanan and Tullock, *The Calculus of Consent*; Becker, A theory of competition among pressure groups. Laffont and Tirole, The politics of government decision-making; Johnson and Libecap, Information distortion and competitive remedies.

alternative to central regulation that he associated with Pigou.[26] As such, he outlined a way of privatizing the externality problem through decentralized exchange. Demsetz reiterated Coase's arguments and criticized the willingness of economists to advocate state intervention. Both Coase's and Demsetz's criticisms relied upon the relatively lower transaction costs of private bargaining compared to government solutions.[27]

The market framework suggested by Coase involved recognizing the reciprocal nature of externalities and the importance of weighing opportunity costs across alternative ways of addressing them: "What has to be decided is whether the gain from preventing the harm is greater than the loss which would be suffered elsewhere as a result of stopping the action which produces the harm."[28] Coase called for shifting attention from market failure to examining the transaction costs reasons for why externalities appeared in the first place. He was interested in what might be done to close externalities through the potentially lower costs of adopting property rights and exchange to address them. His implied policy solution was for government to reduce those costs where feasible rather than adopting prescriptive controls.

Coase pointed out that externalities and their remedies imposed mutual costs on polluters and pollutees. This created a setting whereby negotiation among the parties could lead to resolution as one party compensated the other for changes in production or behavior. Negotiation required the assignment and exchange of economic property rights (the right to be free of pollution or the right to produce and emit pollution). Coase argued that the assignment of the rights should be based on maximizing the value of overall economic production and trade.

---

[26] The absence of Pigouvian taxes is addressed in Buchanan, J. M., and Tullock, G. (1975). Polluters' profits and political response: Direct controls versus taxes. *American Economic Review*, 65: 139–147; and in Keohane et al., The choice of regulatory instruments.

[27] Demsetz, The core disagreement; Pigou, *The Economics of Welfare*; Bator, The anatomy of market failure, 358; Baumol, On taxation and the control of externalities.

[28] Coase, The problem of social cost, 27.

The fundamental virtue of using a market instead of a state response to externalities was that the former revealed willingness-to-pay and willingness-to-accept and would lead to a more complete equalization of marginal costs and benefits in the remediation process. Payments by either party, depending on the assignment of property rights, would reduce the gap between social and private costs associated with externalities. With imposed taxes or regulatory mandates, however, there would be no similar information generated nor political incentive for equating the marginal costs and benefits of environmental controls.

Coase argued that standard government intervention already *implicitly* assigned a property right that had not existed previously. The economic problem was to address externalities where possible and to avoid more serious aggregate harm. Overall economic welfare could be advanced in some cases by allowing the polluting activity to proceed possibly in a limited manner or avoiding subsidizing any alleged positive outcomes. Indeed, according to Coase, there would be cases where the most efficient response would be *to do nothing*. He argued: "But the reason why some activities are not the subject of contracts is exactly the same reason why some contracts are commonly unsatisfactory – it would cost too much to put the matter right."[29]

Coase stated: "When an economist is comparing alternative social arrangements, the proper procedure is to compare the total social product yielded by those different arrangements."[30] The traditional assignment of an implied property right in a policy, such as in the polluter-pays principle, could make society worse off. Coase implicitly asked for consideration of institutions that could lower the costs of defining and enforcing informal and formal property rights, so that exchange could result in mitigation of the externality. He assumed incentives for trade, but did not examine who would be motivated to take such actions or how rent-seeking might displace demand for tradable property rights.

---

[29] Coase, The problem of social cost, 39.
[30] Coase, The problem of social cost, 34.

In a rent-seeking setting, however, politicians, bureaucratic officials, and members of lobby groups typically do not have property rights to the resource. As such they are not the direct residual claimants to added rents generated from market exchange or to the costs imposed by taxes or regulation. Accordingly, government policy makers can make decisions that generate broad social losses in the same way as private parties do when private and social costs differ. There can be externalities in both cases.[31]

## 2.5 TIMING OF INSTITUTIONAL SCHOLARSHIP

It seems unlikely to be a coincidence that literatures tying economic property rights, contracts, and markets to superior economic outcomes appeared in the latter part of the twentieth century as indicated in Figure 2.1. This was also a time of a lingering legacy of New Deal policies to correct alleged market weaknesses, an appeal that appears once again in the environmental policies adopted after 1970 outlined in the Chapter 3. Among influential economists, such as Bator, Samuelson, and Baumol, there was a sense that markets were characterized by failure – monopoly pricing, environmental externalities, short-term profit preoccupation, underinvestment, and inequities.[32] The potential for stagnation and misdirected economic activities called for extensive intervention by government for correction. This concern about market performance occurred when there was a global challenge to western capitalism from state ownership and economic planning in the USSR. A reference to centralized New Deal government intervention is made by Orford as motivation for the Clean Air Act and other federal environmental policies discussed in Chapter 4.[33]

A justification for using industrial policy to advance economic growth earlier was made by economic historian W. W. Rostow,

---

[31] Libecap, G. D. (2016). Coasean bargaining to address environmental externalities, *NBER Working Paper*, No. 21903. January. National Bureau of Economic Research.
[32] Samuelson, P. A. (1954). The pure theory of public expenditure. *Review of Economics and Statistics*, 36 (4): 387–389.
[33] Orford, A. D. (2021). The Clean Air Act of 1963: Postwar environmental politics and the debate over federal power. *Hastings Environmental Law Journal*, 27 (2), Article 2: 1–77.

who was National Security Advisor to President Lyndon Johnson. He described how a market economy required government effort to advance economic growth and to successfully compete with state-owned economies aligned with the Soviet Union. He laid out a comprehensive argument for government action in the economy in *The Stages of Economic Growth: A Non-communist Manifesto*.[34]

Rostow identified five economic conditions in the process of economic growth: (1) Traditional society; (2) Preconditions to take-off; (3) Take-off; (4) Drive to maturity; and (5) Age of high mass consumption. He argued that there was no guarantee that a society based on markets would advance across all five stages. The most likely outcome was for a society to be stuck in one of the stages and to languish there. The remedy was Keynesian-style intervention and industrial policy. Politicians and bureaucratic officials would identify a leading sector, otherwise neglected by the private market, and promote it with subsidies, competitive protections, and other favorable regulatory policies. With this nudge an economy could take off and move across the five stages of growth.

The leading sector would spin off forward and backward linkages, stimulating broad economic growth. To illustrate his arguments, Rostow pointed to the Industrial Revolution in Britain and in the US, to railroads and their alleged transformative role in nineteenth-century US economic expansion. Railroads had been granted favorable state charters as well as land grants from the federal government to build networks across the continent that helped them expand and eventually outcompete local water-based transport. Railroads required iron rails, locomotives, cars, coal, roadbed ties, and other infrastructure, generating huge macroeconomic demand. They lowered transportation and storage costs and promoted the spread of people, information, products, and production across the country.

---

[34] Rostow, W. W. (1960). *The Stages of Economic Growth: A Non-communist Manifesto*. Cambridge University Press.

Rostow argued that the forward and backward linkages from the railroads propelled the American economy across the nineteenth and early twentieth centuries. His conclusion was that state-directed involvement in the economy was essential for economic progress. The pattern could be replicated across the world with US economic aid to generate high levels of growth and welfare, outcompeting communist economies. Rostow did not stress property rights or other institutional bases for markets but rather assumed that economies would coalesce around the leading sector. He also assumed economically beneficial behavior by politicians and agency officials in contrast to the arguments made later by North.[35]

Two challenges were raised to Rostow's arguments. One was empirical. Robert Fogel tested the railroads-as-leading sector hypothesis.[36] He developed a counterfactual of a US economy without railroads and more canals. Given that most agriculture and population in the nineteenth century were in the relatively flat central and eastern US, canal expansion was feasible, and most farmland and population centers would fall within an expanded canal network. Fogel found that railroads were *not* an indispensable leading sector. Comparing the 1890 cost of shipment of agricultural products with and without the railroad, he estimated that the cost differential was below 5 percent of GDP with the difference even less in the 1850s. Further, there were few significant backward linkages during the period 1840–1860. Finally, Fogel did not find evidence of unique discontinuities in the economy that would occur with a stages-of-growth pattern.[37]

---

[35] North, Institutions, transaction costs, and economic growth.

[36] Fogel, R. W. (1962). A quantitative approach to the study of railroads in American economic growth: A report of some preliminary findings. *Journal of Economic History*, 22 (2): 163–197; (1964). *Railroads and American Economic Growth: Essays in Econometric History*. Johns Hopkins Press.

[37] In subsequent analysis using county level data, Donaldson and Hornbeck find a larger market-access effect of the railroad in 1890 on agricultural land values that could not be easily mitigated by feasible extension of the canal network or county roads. Donaldson, D., and Hornbeck, R. (2016). Railroads and American economic growth: A "Market Access" approach. *Quarterly Journal of Economics*, 131 (2): 799–858.

The second criticism of Rostow was based upon a mix of observed endogenous institutional innovation and related economic performance outlined by Douglass North and others.[38] They found a long-term, generally continuous process of US economic growth in the nineteenth century that was not characterized by discrete stages of development due to railroad investments or other lumpy factors. Additionally, Davis and North argued that secure property rights, a stable legal structure, broad access to capital and resource markets, private investment in human and physical capital, along with reduced transportation costs were more important than any leading sector in propelling the American economy forward.[39]

North and Thomas, North, and North and Weingast went beyond the US to explain differences in historical economic growth between England and Holland on the one hand and France and Spain on the other, as well as within England more specifically. They did not find a role for politically designed industrial policies, but rather focused on property rights refinement and security, along with expanded market access.[40] Their analyses indicated that Rostow's imperative for government intervention was misplaced, similar to Coase's more specific challenge to centralized regulation of externalities. North and co-authors showed the potential for market responses to advance welfare in the broad processes of economic growth much as Coase argued for advancing welfare through exchange in the narrower choices of regulatory policy.

## 2.6 CONCLUSION

The objective of this chapter has been to place the analyses of Coase and Pigou and US environmental policies into the broader context of

---

[38] North, *Structure and Change in Economic History*; (1990). *Institutions, Institutional Change and Economic Performance*. Cambridge University Press.
[39] Davis, L. E., and North, D. C. (1971). *Institutional Change and American Economic Growth*. Cambridge University Press.
[40] North and Thomas, *The Rise of the Western World*; North, *Structure and Change in Economic History*; North, D. C., and Weingast, B. (1989). Constitutions and commitment: The evolution of institutions governing public choice in seventeenth-century England. *Journal of Economic History*, 49 (4): 803–832.

the institutional economics literature. Environmental programs and the ways in which the US has addressed externalities since the 1970s are used to illustrate the process of institutional formation. As will be shown in the next chapters, things can stray from the efficient, welfare-enhancing outcomes described as possible in the literature.

Coase used externality mitigation as a way of advancing a simple property rights and exchange framework to confront a standard market failure argument. He and Demsetz countered that externalities were not evidence of market failure, but of incomplete property rights and markets. Recognizing these shortcomings suggested remedies, but, as we will see, these remedies have generally not been followed. Relying upon negotiated exchange might be the low-cost response, as Coase argued. Or it might not be. The answer would depend on a comparison of relative transaction costs, something that Coase explicitly advocated. While the environmental economics literature has criticized Coasean approaches as being irrelevant, it has largely missed that point.[41] Coase did not provide an agenda for adoption but suggested a way of more effectively and efficiently reacting to externalities. Coase's alternative was transparent about costs and benefits and thus generated the information needed to evaluate which method was most beneficial for social welfare.

The neglect of Coasean approaches and reliance instead upon command-and-control intervention imposes potential welfare costs as indicated in subsequent chapters.[42] The nature of these costs is more clearly understood when rent-seeking in the political arena underlying environmental policies is recognized. This appreciation is also largely missing in the environmental economics literature that focuses on public goods provision. The literature lacks models of political behavior and tests of when public goods will be provided

---

[41] Medema, The Coase theorem at sixty.
[42] Important insights are provided in Dixit, A. K. (1996). *The Making of Economic Policy: A Transaction-Cost Politics Perspective*. MIT Press, incorporates transaction cost incentives in policy development to explain the apparent dominance of seemingly inefficient outcomes. He does not fully address the differential incentives of political agents to capture such efficiencies, relative to private market settings.

as compared to when they will be compromised by private, more narrow benefit provision.

The following chapter outlines broader patterns of adoption or lack of adoption of economic property rights worldwide and in fisheries in particular. The discussion then turns to US environmental policies implemented since 1970. As noted earlier, *none* are primarily Coasean and the question arises, why? Chapters 4 through 6 probe the legislative histories of the Clean Air Act Amendments of 1970, 1977, and 1990; US fishery policies under the Magnuson-Stevens Act of 1976; and regulatory mandates to protect at-risk species under the ESA of 1973. The aim is to see first, why Coasean approaches that predated these programs and seemingly are so attractive have not prevailed, and second to explore their resulting costs.

# 3 Economic Property Rights

*Adoption Worldwide and in US Environmental and Natural Resource Policy*

> Commerce and manufactures can seldom flourish long in any state which does not enjoy a regular administration of justice, in which the people do not feel themselves secure in the possession of their property ...
>
> Adam Smith, *The Wealth of Nations*.[1]
>
> The central issue of economic history and of economic development is to account for the evolution of political and economic institutions that create an economic environment that induces increasing productivity.
>
> D. C. North, Institutions.[2]
>
> It was not Coase's observations on the importance of transaction cost but his "privatization" of the externality problem that constitutes the main methodological advance in his work ...
>
> Coase was guided toward privatization of the interaction between parties by his refusal to accept Pigou's and the professions idealized State as a solver of the externality question.
>
> H. Demsetz, The core disagreement.[3]

## 3.1 INTRODUCTION: OVERVIEW

Economic property rights and markets bring transaction costs efficiencies for firms, for the economy, and for addressing

---

[1] Smith, Adam. (1776). *The Wealth of Nations*, book 5, chapter 3, para. 7.
[2] North, D. C. (1991). Institutions. *Journal of Economic Perspectives*, 5 (1): 97–112. 98.
[3] Demsetz, The core disagreement between Pigou, the profession, and Coase in the analyses of the externality question. *European Journal of Political Economy*, 12: 565–579, 566.

environmental externalities.⁴ As summarized in Chapters 1 and 2, these institutions redirect assets, promote investment, encourage search for new opportunities, enhance efficiency, inspire new organizational forms, and generally produce long-term welfare improvements.⁵ Demsetz's quotation emphasizes the valuable point that when complete, economic property rights internalize externalities and promote conservation and efficient provision of environmental public goods.

With these advantages in mind, this chapter examines the record of adoption of economic property rights in general and more specifically of Coase's decentralized framework for US environmental policies with attention to the Clean Water Act. Despite the strong arguments in the economics literature over the past sixty years, these property institutions have not been implemented as extensively as their broad welfare advantages seemingly merited. This is not due to high transaction costs as some have asserted, but more likely because of the opportunities for rent-seeking in the political arena.⁶

---

⁴ Coase, The problem of social cost; Demsetz, The exchange and enforcement of property rights; Demsetz, H. (1966). Some aspects of property rights. *Journal of Law and Economics*, 9 (October): 61–70; Demsetz, Toward a theory of property rights. Williamson, *Markets and Hierarchies*; *The Economic Institutions of Capitalism*; *The Mechanisms of Governance*; and Transaction cost economics. North, D. C. (1990). *Institutions, Institutional Change, and Economic Performance*. Cambridge University Press; Institutions, 111.

⁵ As described in Chapter 2, there was an outpouring of work on property rights and economic growth in the latter part of the twentieth and early twenty-first centuries. See, for example, Acemoglu, D., Johnson, S., and Robinson, J. A. (2002). Reversal of fortune: Geography and institutions in the making of the modern world income distribution. *Quarterly Journal of Economics*, 117 (4): 1231–1294; Rodrik, D., Subramanian, A., and Trebbi, F. (2004). Institutions rule: The primacy of institutions over geography and integration in economic development. *Journal of Economic Growth*, 9 (2): 131–165; Acemoglu, D., and Johnson, S. (2005). Unbundling institutions. *Journal of Political Economy*, 113 (5): 949–995; De Soto, H. (2003). *The Mystery of Capital: Why Capitalism Triumphs in the West and Fails Everywhere Else*. Basic Books; La Porta, R., Lopez-De-Silanes, F., Shleifer, A., and Vishny, R.W. (1998). Law and finance. *Journal of Political Economy*, 106 (6): 1113–1155.

⁶ Schmalensee and Stavins argue that the costs of establishing property rights to clean air limited use of Coasean approaches in the Clean Air Act of 1970 and its amendments of 1977 and 1990; Schmalensee, R., and Stavins, R. N. (2019). Policy evolution under the Clean Air Act. *Journal of Economic Perspectives*, 33 (4): 27–50. Medema,

Alternative political/economic institutions affected by rent-seeking reduce both the demand for and supply of economic property rights and markets. Rent-seeking has negative economic and social consequences for the overall economy and as laid out in the volume, for effectively and equitably addressing environmental externalities.[7]

## 3.2 THE GENERAL EMPIRICAL RECORD OF ECONOMIC PROPERTY RIGHTS

Figure 3.1 provides a map of economic property rights extent and security worldwide based on aggregate index measures in 2024. The index data and map are provided by the Property Rights Alliance and are available online.[8] The extent and security of economic property rights is revealed by shading, where countries with the most secure institutions are shaded light grey, such as Finland (highest index score), and those with the least secure property rights shaded dark, such as Venezuela (lowest index score).[9] Those countries with no shading lack relevant data. The map reveals that for much of the world, stable, relatively complete, transferable private property rights do not exist. The question arises, why is this the case in light of their potential aggregate welfare benefits?

Figure 3.2 shows that the pattern of property rights adoption is mirrored in measures of economic performance per capita. The data are compiled by the International Monetary Fund (IMF) for 2022 from the agency's World Economic Outlook in constant dollars and are available online. The shading traces those countries with the highest per capita GDP as dark and those with lower income levels with

---

The Coase theorem at sixty. Tullock, The welfare costs of tariffs, monopolies and theft; *The Rent-Seeking Society*; Krueger, The political economy of the rent-seeking society.

[7] Acemoglu and Robinson, *Why Nations Fail*; North et al., *Violence and Social Orders*. See also, Johnson, Disease environments; Acemoglu, Institutions, technology and prosperity; and Robinson, Paths towards the periphery.

[8] https://internationalpropertyrightsindex.org/countries.

[9] Property Rights Alliance, *2024 International Property Rights Index: Countries*. https://internationalpropertyrightsindex.org/countries.

48    3 ECONOMIC PROPERTY RIGHTS

FIGURE 3.1 World property rights extent and security.
*Note:* Country categories are based on a numerical index of property rights security. The very light shaded countries, such as Libya, have no information and are not ranked. For other countries, such as the US, Canada, Australia, the light gray shading indicates a more secure rights system. Darker gray as for Brazil and Argentina, indicate weaker internal property rights. The darkest shading as for the Russian Federation, Iran, and Venezuela, indicate relatively weak property rights security and protection. Countries without data are shown in white. See the Property Rights Alliance, 2024 International Property Rights Index for discussion, https://internationalpropertyrightsindex.org/.
*Source:* Access granted from International Property Rights Index.

gradually lighter shading. For instance, using 2025 data, the US had $89,680 GDP per capita and Canada with $55,800, shown as dark in Figure 3.2 for 2022, whereas Brazil had $10,820, Iran $5,300, and Egypt $3,160, as shown as lighter in the figure for 2022.[10] In countries where economic property rights and markets are prevalent and the state sector has a smaller share of GNP (not explicitly shown), economies perform more effectively with greater individual economic welfare.[11] Although the comparisons of aggregate maps are not

---

[10] IMF. (2025). *World Economic Outlook.* www.imf.org/external/datamapper/NGDPDPC @WEO/OEMDC/ADVEC/WEOWORLD.

[11] See La Porta et al., Law and finance; La Porta et al., The economic consequences of legal origins; La Porta, R., Lopez-de-Silanes, F., Shleifer, A., and Vishny, R. W. (1997). Legal determinants of external finance. *Journal of Finance*, 52: 1131–1150. There are

## 3.2 EMPIRICAL RECORD OF ECONOMIC PROPERTY RIGHTS 49

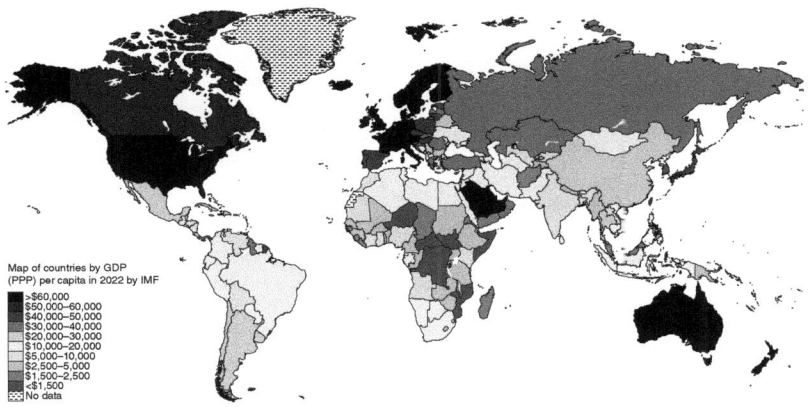

FIGURE 3.2 World per capita GDP.
*Source:* Wikipedia. https://tinyurl.com/mtxzzwdz.

statistical analyses, the relationships are unmistakable. Countries with the least robust property rights institutions and market activities are also those with the lowest GDP per capita. This observation also reflects the causal relationship suggested by North.[12]

If one turns to the adoption of property rights and exchange to address externalities, the record surprisingly is similar despite theory and long-term experience. For example, property rights are the most obvious solution to open access and associated losses from the race to fish. The remedy has long been understood, predating Coase.[13] Indeed, the property rights solution in fisheries management was outlined extensively in 1973 by Christy through secure, exchangeable shares of a total allowable catch (cap-and-trade). The background

---

various measures of the size of the state sector, including employment, ownership of resources, expenditures, or tax revenues. One approach is in Hall, R. E. (2009). By how much does GDP rise if the government buys more output? *Brookings Papers on Economic Activity, Economic Studies Program*, The Brookings Institution, 40 (2): 183–249.

[12] These points are emphasized in Johnson, Disease environments; Acemoglu, Institutions, technology and prosperity; and Robinson, Paths towards the periphery. North, Institutions, transaction costs, and economic growth.

[13] Gordon, H. S. (1954). The economic theory of a common-property resource: The fishery. *Journal of Political Economy*, 62 (2): 124–142. Scott, The fishery.

## 50  3 ECONOMIC PROPERTY RIGHTS

FIGURE 3.3 Global fisheries managed with property rights.
Source: Costello, C., Lynham, J., Lester, S. E., and Gaines, S. D. (2010). Economic incentives and global fisheries sustainability. *Annual Review of Resource Economics*, 2 (1): 299–318, figure 1. Access granted via Copyright Marketplace 1-28-2025.

to Christy's work was the even more longstanding framework laid out in 1911 by Jens Warming.[14] Catch shares or quotas as individual tradable quotas (ITQs) were adopted in 1975 onward in New Zealand, Iceland, and regions of the US and Canada after prescriptive input and output controls failed to halt the race to fish. Even so, while the losses of competitive access are universal, most countries have not embraced ITQs, as shown in Figure 3.3.[15]

The Figure provides a map of global fishery property rights and does not include the many nuances within and across them. For example, within the US, fishery property rights were implemented late and in very abbreviated ways across the country's many fisheries, undermining their efficiency potential and lowering their economic values. Nevertheless, around the world, where fishery management

---

[14] Christy, F. T. (1973). Fisherman quotas: A tentative suggestion for domestic management. *Occasional Papers*, No. 19, Law Sea Institute, University of Rhode Island. Warming, J. (1911). Om Grundrente af Fiskegrunde (On rent of fishing grounds). *Nation-alökonomisk Tidsskrift*, 49: 499–505.
[15] World Bank et al., *Sunken Billions*.

exists, centralized controls dominate in regulated fisheries with enormous wastes. More alarmingly, many countries' fisheries remain relatively open access.

Again, why do we see such surprisingly limited adoption of property rights in general and for fishery rights in particular? Are there lessons from the pattern of environmental regulations for institutional formation more generally?

To get a better sense of the impediments to valuable institutional formation, the next section examines US environmental policies enacted since 1970 to address externalities, Coase's focus in 1960. As pointed out earlier, Coase used externality as a means of illustrating the efficiency and welfare gains of adopting property rights and relying upon decentralized trade for mitigation rather than on prescriptive intervention.

## 3.3 US ENVIRONMENTAL LAWS

### Overview: Where Is Coase? Why Is He Missing? What Has Been Lost?

As acknowledged in Chapter 1, there is an analytical challenge in comparing actual policies that have observed provisions with hypothetical decentralized Coasean ones. Coase is never adopted as the primary, early response to externalities in US environmental policies, while prescriptive mandates are dominant in all. Accordingly, there can be no clear, one-for-one comparison, only suggestions as to what might have been possible with a property rights and market institutional framework rather than command and control.

For some, a comparison of theoretical Coase with actual regulatory policies will not be credible because the transaction costs underlying a Coasean approach have not been considered. That is a fair criticism because the assignment and exchange of property rights between polluters and pollutees under Coase would entail costs, especially for multilateral, broader range, mobile resources, and related externalities. The response here is that government remedies also involve transaction costs that could be greater. The interaction among the EPA, various lobby groups, members of Congress, the President, and the courts around provisions of the Clean Air Act discussed in the following chapter suggests that observed policy-based transaction costs could be substantial. Moreover, as stated earlier, the legislative histories examined later in the volume do not reveal a comparison of transaction costs with decentralized or centralized externality mitigation in policy selection. Observed environmental policy apparently was not chosen because of its relative efficiencies.

Government environmental policies also might have focused on how to implement Coasean approaches by lowering transaction costs, instead of implementing centralized prescriptive regulation. They do not do that. Again, the question is why? Moreover, as we will see transaction costs did not block defining rights to migrating fish stocks once the US decided to do so around 1996; the tradable right to pollute in the Acid Rain Program after 1990; or in the Regional Clean Air Incentives Market (RECLAIM) in southern California after 1994.[16] The cap was not negotiated in those cases as they would have been with Coase, but rights were established, and trading occurred. There is no obvious reason why the cap could not have been determined by the parties involved or why property rights to environmental resources might not have been defined.

A summary of US environmental policies is not a criticism of them nor a dismissal of their benefits. Instead, it is an overview of how and why they do not incorporate Coasean approaches as their framework and what is lost as a result. Limited cap-and-trade policies are added late in some of the programs, but those do not represent a restructuring of US externality restrictions, except in a very complex manner in US fisheries. Rather, these incentive policies are segments of overall regulation, along their peripheries, and do not represent a major shift in mitigation efforts to reflect the general efficiency benefits Coase outlined.

[16] www.aqmd.gov/home/programs/business/business-detail?title=reclaim.

So then, why not Coase? The answer, as we have stressed, is the attraction of rents to politicians, agency officials, environmental NGO members, industry representatives, labor unions, as well as some natural scientists and academics. These parties achieve pecuniary and nonpecuniary programmatic benefits at low direct cost. Nonpecuniary normative objectives are particularly common in environmental issues, where individuals have strongly held opinions and aims and want them implemented by the state without paying a commensurate share of the costs involved. Through command and control, advocates achieve the certainty of single government mandates, largely paid for by others, relative to messier negotiated outcomes that would require market payments. One can think of these as government-provided consumer surplus. Centralized regulations also can be used to advance politically favored commercial or pecuniary positions. These are examples of government-provided producer surplus generated by raising rivals' costs and restricting entry. Moreover, property rights and trade as an alternative would reduce the role of politicians, agency officials, and lobbyists in externality mitigation. Abatement would be negotiated between polluters and pollutees, not dictated via the political process.

As argued before, prescriptive public goods provision does not allow for easy analysis of marginal costs and benefits due to measurement problems and importantly, a lack of incentives among parties involved to engage in it. Such cost/benefit analysis is, however, explicit in market exchange. Accordingly, under command and control there is potential for excess environmental regulation, where marginal social costs exceed marginal benefits, notwithstanding the presence of public goods. As suggested earlier, when policy costs become too high relative to delivered benefits and if the distributional effects become too transparent, then collective action by citizens may mobilize as a remedy. Unfortunately, many costs may have already been inflicted and not be easily overcome.

Rents occur because politics and related externality regulation by the state are less open to access and competitive revision than is the case with property rights and markets. Indeed, political rents would be less attractive if they could be easily *competed away* via entry. Once environmental policies are put into place with associated rent distributions, constituencies form and resist any major readjustment. By contrast, markets undermine entrenched hierarchies and existing cost/benefit distributions. If property rights and exchange are feasible, agents can respond to air, water, and land-use externalities and adjust them as conditions change.[17] Only fishery regulation of US environmental laws has moved seriously toward incentive-based settings, displacing previous controls. Those regulations had so completely failed that property rights and markets became politically feasible. Even then, however, the property rights offered were molded by rent-seeking to direct them to favored constituencies and to limit entry.

For some the very existence of externalities indicates the inability of localities or states to successfully confront alleged market failure, generating an imperative for federal government intervention.[18] While plausible, the basis for such claims is unclear. First, there is little empirical evidence of failure to address externalities. Observed pollution may reflect the levels desired by local organizations and citizens who must weigh tradeoffs. Externality control is costly, and some tradeoffs may be just too great. What does failure mean? What is the baseline comparison for such assertions? Zero pollution?

Second, while there are demands by some constituencies for more federal government intervention regarding the environment, it

---

[17] Private conservation efforts are reflected in conservation easements voluntarily adopted by landowners and fee-simple acquisitions, for example. See the efforts of the Nature Conservancy. www.nature.org/en-us/about-us/who-we-are/how-we-work/private-lands-conservation/. Fisher and Dills quantitatively examine private land-use conservation in Fisher, J. R. B., and Dills, B. (2012). Do private conservation activities match science-based conservation priorities? *Plos One*. September 28, 2012, doi .org/10.1371/journal.pone.0046429.

[18] For example, see reference to market failure in externalities as justification for Clean Air Act controls in McCarthy, J. E., and Lattanzio, R. K. (2017). Cost and benefit considerations in Clean Air Act Regulations. Congressional Research Service 2017. R44840, p. 10. https://crsreports.congress.gov.

is not obvious how broad and deep that support may be relative to more narrow interest group efforts.[19] As argued here, for some, government mandates provide privately desired environmental controls at low direct cost, which is rent-seeking. This is not to say that public goods have not been provided. They have, but plausibly at higher cost than more local decentralized responses might entail. Moreover, decentralized actions more likely involve implicit balancing of marginal social costs and benefits than broader command and control, influenced by rent-seeking by national groups.

This issue is addressed more specifically in Chapter 4 for the Clean Air Act. Commonly referenced surveys surrounding US environmental regulation may not be accurate indicators of general citizen support because respondents do not have to bear actual costs in their responses. Further, unless questionnaires outline a range of options, including Coasean approaches, one cannot conclude that federal regulation would have been the primary choice. Indeed, there may be no general constituencies across the population willing to pay their actual share of the costs and support observed levels of regulation, unless the direct costs and related tradeoffs are not made readily apparent to survey respondents.[20]

## US Environmental Laws

The focus of the volume is on the Clean Water Act, the Clean Air Act, the Magnuson-Stevens Fishery Management Act, and the Endangered Species Act. In general, across the range of US environmental laws there is little that is Coasean. The main thrust of all the legislation

---

[19] The rise of environmental NGOs and the overall environmental movement is discussed by Coglianese, C. (2001). Social movements, law, and society: The institutionalization of the environmental movement. *University of Pennsylvania Law Review*, 150: 85–118. For discussion of the issues involved in interpreting poll data, see Berinsky, A. J. (2017). Measuring public opinion with surveys. *Annual Review of Political Science*, 20: 309–329.

[20] In a contemporary setting, see Citizen Campaign for the Environment, www.citizenscampaign.org/or, the EPA's online framework for the National Environmental Policy Act. https://shorturl.at/NrE1H. For discussion of the issues involved in interpreting poll data, see Berinsky, Measuring public opinion with surveys.

is centralized regulation, not the assignment of property rights and decentralized exchange between polluters and pollutees. The laws do not entail taxes but are characterized by federal government prescriptive standards and other behavioral constraints along with compliance requirements that include fines and additional penalties for violation.

The Environmental Protection Agency (EPA) was created by Executive Order from President Nixon in 1970. The EPA was assigned overall discretion and authority in drafting, coordinating, and enforcing federal environmental regulations within authorizing statutes that typically are very general and in some cases very short.[21] The agency publishes proposed rules in the *Federal Register* prior to promulgating them. Advocates or opponents can submit comments or file for review in federal courts. By design, the arrangement is very reactive. Under the statutes, the EPA (or other federal agencies, such as the Fish and Wildlife Service, FWS, or National Oceanic and Atmospheric Administration) outline regulations and require that firms, individuals, or other regulated parties adjust to them within predetermined timelines.

US Environmental legislation generally is mired in controversies, and proposed adjustments have been stalemated in Congress.[22] Partisan resistance to associated alleged public goods often is stressed as the reason.[23] But this explanation misses the problem of

---

[21] Schmalensee and Stavins note regarding the Clean Air Act: "This law, only 24 pages in length, gave the EPA considerable discretion and authority to set and change regulations and to enforce compliance." Schmalensee and Stavins, Policy evolution under the Clean Air Act, 28.

[22] Reitze, A. W. Jr. (1999). The legislative history of US air pollution control. *Houston Law Review*, 36: 679–741 at 729. Reitze is discussing the Clean Air Act, but as is emphasized later, this situation also describes the Endangered Species Act. See also Schmalensee and Stavins, Policy evolution under the Clean Air Act, 45–46, for the Clean Air Act. The complete study of differential compliance costs based upon plant vintage and firm regulatory anticipation is provided by Clay, K., Akshaya, J., Lewis, J., and Severnini, E. (2022). Impacts of the Clean Air Act on the power sector from 1938–1994: Anticipation and adaptation, *NBER Working Paper*, No. 28962. National Bureau of Economic Research.

[23] Orford points to industry opposition to the 1963 Clean Air Act. Orford, The Clean Air Act of 1963, 64–65.

disproportionate distributions of costs and benefits, inherent in the command-and-control mandates without commensurate compensation that generate intense political reaction pro and con.

## Institutional Frameworks for Collaborative Externality Mitigation

Coase, Demsetz, and Cheung point to the source of externality as poorly defined property rights.[24] Indeed, Schmalensee and Stavins conclude that: "If resources such as clean air could be recognized as a form of property, with corresponding rights that could be traded in a market, private actors could allocate the use of this property in a cost-effective way."[25]

Stavins and Schmalensee did not examine these costs, but property rights seemingly could have been created to address externalities. If they did not exist for decentralized exchange, federal, state, and local governments as well as the judiciary might have provided a framework for establishing and exchanging them.[26] All government levels and agencies could have supported basic research on externality costs as a basis for market negotiation. The legal system could have enforced contracts and addressed compliance. As outlined in Chapter 4, the initial focus of the Clean Air Act was on local, intrastate pollution, where the number and heterogeneity of the parties would have been less than interstate, a setting with lower transaction costs and presumably allowing for decentralized bargaining.

Moreover, as noted in Chapter 1, many institutional options have existed as templates for addressing externalities, had a more collaborative approach been the objective. Local or regional organizations might have been formed, such as a homeowners' association or groundwater conservation district, to provide a stage for identifying externalities, supporting abatement negotiation, and providing

---

[24] Cheung, The structure of a contract; Demsetz, The core disagreement.
[25] Schmalensee and Stavins, Policy evolution under the Clean Air Act, 33.
[26] There are long-standing approaches to property rights assignment. See Lueck, The rule of first possession.

enforcement.[27] Negotiations would have involved distributing property rights among potential polluters and pollutees, setting the pollution cap, and creating an institutional structure for exchange. A more cooperative, flexible, and less costly arrangement than the observed centralized approach might have been put into place and likely have been welfare improving.[28]

## Example of Prescriptive Regulation: The Clean Water Act

To illustrate how far federal environmental regulation deviates from a decentralized, Coasean approach, consider the Clean Water Act of 1972 (33 USC 1251), the country's primary water pollution control law. The infamous fire on the surface of the Cuyahoga River in Cleveland, June 22, 1969, sparked protests and calls by some for national water pollution controls. The most well-known photograph of the river's potential for fire is shown in Figure 3.4, which details an effort by firemen on November 3, 1952 to spray water on the tug *Arizona*, as a fire, started in an oil slick on the river, swept the docks at the Great Lakes. Although the events have been used as a rallying call for centralized environmental action, that did not have to be the response. It generated political pressure from a variety of political advocates for Congressional responses,

---

[27] Ellickson, R. C. (1982). Cities and homeowners associations. *University of Pennsylvania Law Review*, 130: 1519; Edwards, E. C. (2016). What lies beneath? Aquifer heterogeneity and the economics of groundwater management. *Journal of the Association of Environmental and Resource Economists*, 3 (2): 453–491. Mulligan, C. B. (2023). Beyond Pigou: Externalities and civil society in the supply–demand framework. *Public Choice*, 196: 1–18.

[28] Schmalensee and Stavins discuss the Acid Rain and RECLAIM programs (Schmalensee and Stavins, Policy evolution under the Clean Air Act, 36–40). Hann had a more optimistic assessment of the potential for Coasean approaches and the role of economists in environmental policies. He lists various cap-and-trade programs at the federal and state level. He wrote at a time of optimism that more recent evidence likely does not support. As environmental programs have received more political attention, become more constraining, and received far more funding, the opportunities for rent-seeking and political property have grown. Prescriptive mandates remain dominant. See Hahn, R. W. (1999). The impact of economics on environmental policy. *Journal of Environmental Economics and Management*, 39: 375–399.

FIGURE 3.4 Cuyahoga River, Cleveland, Ohio, June 22, 1969.
*Source:* Courtesy of WKYC Studios: https://shorturl.at/KtdgV.

ultimately leading to passage of the Clean Water Act within three years.[29] The fire indicated a buildup of pollution, and it might have been addressed by the communities immediately affected. It certainly provided dramatic information about pollution levels and the threats they posed. Coordinated efforts among local and regional governments, citizen groups, industry, and labor unions for mitigation could have been mobilized. While the fire was a call to action, it did not have to be federal action. The parties, information, and incentives for weighing the benefits and costs of new controls were far more local.

Indeed, many US water bodies (streams, ponds, lakes) abut fairly limited land areas and involve local populations. Decentralized negotiations regarding use and pollution controls seemingly were

[29] Coglianese, Social movements, law, and society.

feasible. Water pollution and the costs and benefits of addressing it would be addressed by immediate entities, facilitating potentially low-cost exchange. Polluters and pollutees typically could identify one another; define property rights; and negotiate controls on discharges that reflected current conditions and tradeoffs. Resulting negotiated pollution levels might have been greater or less than observed national quality standards under the EPA. For less common cross-boundary water sources, quality and other management issues are addressed by interstate water compacts. These compacts might have provided a framework for broader coordination rather than federalizing the issue.[30]

This is not the approach of the Clean Water Act as enacted in 1972. National water quality standards are drafted to "maintain the chemical, physical and biological integrity of the Nation's waters."[31] These criteria are used by states, territories, and tribal governments to define targeted quality levels that must be approved by the agency. The EPA can promulgate federal water quality standards if it determines that state standards are inconsistent with the national targets under the Clean Water Act. EPA regulations apply to pollution discharges from point sources – industrial and municipal wastewater treatment facilities.[32] The agency also sets antidegradation requirements to restrict deterioration of water quality that already is above recommended standards. Permitting of facilities might be denied or conditional operation permits granted to point sources, and mitigation responses monitored.[33] As with No Significant Deterioration rules under the Clean Air Act, this rule could have economic

---

[30] Examples include the Colorado River Compact, 1922; the Republican River Compact, 1942; and the Rio Grande Compact of 1938.

[31] www.epa.gov/wqs-tech/what-are-water-quality-standards.

[32] www.epa.gov/history/epa-history-federal-water-pollution-control-act-amendments-1972.

[33] Adler argues that under the Clean Water Act, negotiated settlements on water quality effectively are precluded: Adler, J. H. (2001). Stand or deliver: Citizen suites, standing, and environmental protection. *Duke Environmental Law and Policy Forum*, 12: 39–84.

consequences if local citizens sought greater industrial production, employment, and income that would raise pollution, even if water quality remained high relative to the national standard.

Tradable water-quality discharge permits within the uniform standards were authorized in 2003 to make the controls more economically rational. This resort to Coase, over *thirty* years after the Clean Water Act was passed, not only suggests the high costs involved under the legislation, but also its relative ineffectiveness in some situations. By 2003, rivers, streams, and lakes often still did not meet suggested national quality targets.[34] Trading was allowed, not to redefine standards economically, but rather to lower the costs of meeting them. If tradable pollution rights could be created then, why not at the beginning of the Clean Water Act?

The risks of mandated political controls under the Clean Water Act explain why agricultural interests have opposed greater coverage of nonpoint sources of water pollution. Nonpoint sources can be primary contributors to water quality degradation. A more open, flexible decentralized approach that included setting pollution caps, property rights, and payments for violation of agreements might have encouraged more active participation by agriculture. There are a variety of ways in which agricultural interests and those concerned about pollution might bargain over controls. Land easements are an example of one negotiated option.[35]

## 3.4 CONCLUSION

The formation of institutions that reduce transaction costs in responding to economic signals and opportunities can bring large welfare improvements. These gains are documented in economic history and development by North and La Porta et al. for economies as

---

[34] www.epa.gov/system/files/documents/2022-12/Water-Quality-Trading-Policy.pdf.

[35] See, for example, Karwowski, (2024). Estimating the effect of easements on agricultural production. In Libecap, G. D., and Dinar, A. eds., *American Agriculture, Water Resources, and Climate Change*. University of Chicago Press, 53–106.

a whole and for firms by Coase and Williamson.[36] Economic property rights and market exchange are fundamental, but often are limited in the US or worldwide.

North et al., Acemoglu and Robinson offer explanations as to why these suboptimal conditions occur and persist.[37] Their analyses focus on the macro level and the role of various groups within societies to limit institutional innovation in order to capture private rents and to enhance their economic and political positions. The approach here is a more micro one, to focus on the framework presented by Coase to efficiently mitigate environmental externalities. Coase used this specific example as a metaphor to describe the advantages of property rights and markets for an economy. He argued that this approach could involve lower transaction costs, be more effective, and generally make society better off. He asserted that one could not automatically draw such conclusions with centralized controls.

Despite this potential, Coase's framework has not been adopted as the principal approach in the US environmental legislation. There are benefits and costs of the observed prescriptive approach, and the costs are likely larger and more inequitably distributed, than with a Coasean decentralized framework. A more detailed examination is provided in key legislative histories in the following chapters.

---

[36] North, D. C. (1981). *Structure and Change in Economic History; Institutions, Institutional Change, and Economic Performance*. North, Institutions; La Porta et al., The economic consequences of legal origins; Coase, The nature of the firm; Williamson, *Markets and Hierarchies; The Economic Institutions of Capitalism; The Mechanisms of Governance*.

[37] North et al., *Violence and Social Orders*; Acemoglu and Robinson, *Why Nations Fail*.

# 4 Transaction Cost Reduction or Rent-Seeking in Provision of a Public Good

*The Clean Air Act*

> The harmful effects of the activities of a business can assume a wide variety of forms … What has to be decided is whether the gain from preventing the harm is greater than the loss which would be suffered elsewhere as a result of stopping the action which produces the harm.
>
> Ronald H. Coase, The problem of social cost.

> There are no solutions. There are only trade-offs.
>
> Thomas T. Sowell, *A Conflict of Visions*.[1]

> Taken together, our research suggests that environmental policy can have large but unequal environmental benefits and economic costs that, even a half century after passage of many environmental laws, we are still working to understand.
>
> J. S. Shapiro and R. Walker, US Environmental Policies.[2]

> The knowledge necessary to administer any air pollution control program-to set implementation and enforcement priorities and to plan for future development-can be found only at the local level. The practical need to tailor implementation and enforcement to local conditions requires decision-makers who have, in addition to an adequate knowledge of these conditions, a sympathetic orientation toward local conditions. Effective implementation requires some consideration and accommodation of local concerns.
>
> J. P. Dwyer, The practice of federalism under the Clean Air Act.[3]

---

[1] Sowell, T. (1987). *A Conflict of Visions: Ideological Origins of Political Struggles*. William Morrow & Co.
[2] Shapiro, J. S., and Walker, R. (2022). US environmental policies, the environment, and the economy. NBER *Reporter*, July 5.
[3] Dwyer, J. P. (1995). The practice of federalism under the Clean Air Act. *Maryland Law Review*, 54 (4), 1183–1225. 1218.

## 4.1 OVERVIEW OF THE CLEAN AIR ACT: DECENTRALIZED RESPONSES OR PRESCRIPTIVE NATIONAL REGULATION WITH RENT-SEEKING IN THE PROVISION OF A PUBLIC GOOD

This chapter reviews the legislative history of the Clean Air Act and the role of rent-seeking in affecting key aspects of the law. These aspects include uniform ambient air quality standards across a large, heterogeneous country; prevention of significant air quality deterioration even in areas above the national standards; and New Source Emission Review that requires best available pollution control technologies in new facilities also in areas with air quality at or above the national standard. These policies might seem reasonable except that they impose costs on sections of the country where there may be little corresponding net benefit. The question then arises as to why the Clean Air Act is structured in this manner. Are there transaction cost savings arising from these rules? Or are they better explained by rent-seeking among politicians, agency officials, industry and labor lobbyists, and environmental NGOs designed to shield parts of the country from industrial competition and to provide psychic or normative values to particular parties? If so, these are producer and consumer surpluses granted to political advocates by law that cannot be easily competed away and may not be easily assessed by general citizens.

In part, rent-seeking is obscured by the large aggregate public goods associated with the Clean Air Act.[4] The EPA has performed cost/benefit analyses and finds that aggregate benefits far outweigh costs.[5] The benefits are largely health improvements

---

[4] Currie, J., and Walker, R. (2019). What do economists have to say about the Clean Air Act 50 Years after the establishment of the Environmental Protection Agency? *Journal of Economic Perspectives*, 33 (4): 3–26; Schmalensee and Stavins, Policy evolution under the Clean Air Act; Aldy et al., Looking back at 50 years of the Clean Air Act.

[5] See https://shorturl.at/5hUAP, where the human health benefits of reducing particulates and ground-level $SO_2$ are the greatest contributors to total benefits. EPA. *The Benefits and Costs of the Clean Air Act from 1990 to 2020 Final Report* – Rev. A U.S. Environmental Protection Agency Office of Air and Radiation April. 2–9.

from reduction of local emissions of particulates and ground-level sulfur dioxide ($SO_2$) from coal-fired industrial facilities and power plants. Cross-boundary emissions as well as those from mobile sources also have been reduced by the limited use of incentive-based instruments.

What was the baseline from which the Clean Air Act launched improvements? Surprisingly, this is not obvious. Although there are claims that prior decentralized efforts were fragmented, incomplete, or "failing," there is no empirical evidence mustered by those who make such assertions except to point to polluted air. While air quality certainly has improved in areas with previous high pollution, current quality levels may be higher than citizens would have desired in light of local cost/benefit tradeoffs. Reducing air pollution has costs, and some areas might have been willing to accept some deterioration in quality as an acceptable tradeoff for more industrial activity and employment. Fragmentation alone is not evidence of failure. It reflects the heterogeneities in costs and benefits of air pollution control across the country.

Figure 4.1 is a map of EPA nonattainment counties, areas that have not met the national standards in at least one controlled pollutant. What is notable is how dispersed nonattainment is, except for southern and central California. The map suggests that local conditions were and are important and that decentralized approaches for improving air quality might have been more effective and optimal compared to nationwide uniform standards and associated requirements. Revesz describes efforts by municipalities and states to reduce local pollution and provides examples in Pittsburgh, Chicago, and Cincinnati, along with some states.[6] He suggests these actions were driven by growing empirical studies of the benefits of lowering concentrations of $SO_2$ and suspended particulates, PM.

---

[6] Revesz, R. L. (2001). Federalism and environmental regulation: A public choice analysis. *Harvard Law Review*, 116 (2): 553–641, 578–584.

FIGURE 4.1 Clean Air Act Uniform Ambient Air Quality Standards Non-attainment Counties.
*Note:* The National Ambient Air Quality Standards (NAAQS) are health standards for carbon monoxide, lead (1978 and 2008), nitrogen dioxide, 8-hour ozone (2008), particulate matter (PM-10 and PM-2.5) (1997, 2006, and 2012), and sulfur dioxide (1971 and 2010). Included in the counts are counties designated for NAAQS and revised NAAQS pollutants. Revoked 1-hour and 8-hour ozone (1997) are excluded. Partial counties, those with part of the county designated nonattainment and part attainment, are shown as full counties on the map.
*Source:* www3.epa.gov/airquality/greenbook/map/mapnmpoll.pdf.

The picture in Figure 4.2 of air pollution from Pittsburgh area factories in the early twentieth century illustrates a baseline from which air quality has improved in the US. Indeed, the historical narrative tied to the picture suggests that those were unhealthy times for Pittsburgh with poor air quality, largely from coal-burning steel production, that endangered the lives of citizens, lowered some

4.1 OVERVIEW OF THE CLEAN AIR ACT 67

FIGURE 4.2 Pittsburgh steel mill emissions, 1925.
*Source:* Holmes I. Mettee, photographer, Carnegie Museum of Art Collection, Fair Use: https://shorturl.at/CGo8E.

property values, and undermined the overall quality of life.[7] In terms of air quality, conditions are much better now. It is not obvious how much of the change is due to the Clean Air Act and how much would

---

[7] Tarr, J. (2003). *Ensuring Environmental Health in Postindustrial Cities: Workshop Summary.* National Academies Press, chapter 3, figure 3.1; (2003). *The Changing Face of Pittsburgh: A Historical Perspective,* Institute of Medicine (US) Roundtable on Environmental Health Sciences, Research, and Medicine. Goldstein, Bernard D., Fischhoff, Baruch, Marcus, Steven J., and Coussens, Christine M. (eds.). National Academies Press.

have occurred with local action. Production and employment have shifted in the region, bringing positive results for many, but possibly not for all.

The costs and benefits of enhanced air quality are unlikely to have been equally distributed across the area's population. While reduced emissions brought documented health gains, any factory or plant closing or migration would have affected employment and career opportunities for existing workers. Pristine air would have required virtually no industrial activity and the employment it provided. It is possible that Clean Air Act restrictions contributed to a change in the industrial structure of Pittsburgh's economy and related job prospects. This outcome also may have affected other parts of the US economy and society where heavy industry historically had been significant. Other factors, such as greater competition from international producers, certainly also played a role. Currie and Walker conclude that the Clean Air Act successfully reduced regulated pollution, but caution that it is not possible to know exactly how much of the reduction over the past fifty years can be attributed solely to the statute.[8]

In the case of Pittsburgh, heavy industry that led to the title "Steel City" declined and moved away. Major sources of employment and contributions to the area's economy are now universities, financial services, and trade, with steelmaking and other heavy industry being less important. As steel mills closed, the number of employees working in the industry fell.[9] Workers in steel production might not

---

[8] Currie and Walker, What do economists have to say about the Clean Air Act.
[9] See the summary statistics in Haller, W. (2005). Industrial restructuring and urban change in the Pittsburgh Region: Developmental, ecological, and socioeconomic tradeoffs. *Ecology and Society*, 10 (1). Extensive discussion of air and water pollution control efforts in Pittsburgh is found in Tarr, *The Changing Face of Pittsburgh*; Muller, E., and Tarr, J. (eds.). (2019). *Making Pittsburgh Modern*. University of Pittsburgh Press. There is little detail in the literature on local pollution control and why it was subsequently declared incomplete or a failure when Congress debated the Clean Air Act. Given that the country had many localities with differing levels of pollution, population, incomes, and industrial structures, it would be possible to systematically analyze local pollution control and the determinants of relative success.

have easily transferred to other occupations, such as services, where skills and locations were different. Built-up human capital values probably were lost, at least for some. Although across industrial US cities Pittsburgh appears to have smoothly transitioned to a less manufacturing-based economy, others, such as Cleveland, Detroit, and Buffalo, may not have been as successful with incumbent falls in population, housing values, and economic activity.[10]

This is not to say that the Clean Air Act was the primary contributor to a decline in industrial activity in historical manufacturing US regions.[11] The point is that the Clean Air Act's uniform national ambient air quality standards and restrictions on internal US plant mobility did not reflect or allow for significant local tradeoff considerations in pollution abatement and industrial production. The law imposed the constraints. It imposed a tax on US production that may have shifted investment decisions on the margin to move out of specific cities and regions.[12]

A common narrative that industry would be opposed to emission controls may also be off the mark. By the 1960s, the health and productivity improvements from cleaner air were becoming better understood. The environmental movement was gaining traction across segments of the US population.[13] Firms could not have been indifferent to these factors for their labor forces and products in competitive labor and product markets. It seems likely that industry and the communities in which they operated would have had joint incentives to lower harmful emissions of particulates.

---

This information would allow for assessing what federal efforts might have allowed for Coasean success as compared with the uniform mandates under the Clean Air Act.

[10] A useful study is by Hartley, D. A. (2013). Urban decline in rust-belt cities. *Economic Commentary*. Federal Reserve Bank of Cleveland, May.

[11] Baily, M. N., and Bosworth, B. P. (2014). US manufacturing: Understanding its past and its potential future. *Journal of Economic Perspectives*, 28 (1): 3–26.

[12] Shapiro, J. S., and Walker, R. (2018). Why is pollution from US manufacturing declining? The roles of environmental regulation, productivity, and trade. *American Economic Review*, 108 (12): 3814–3854.

[13] The rise of environmental NGOs and the overall environmental movement is discussed by Coglianese, Social movements, law, and society.

The additional claim that cross-boundary pollution would have eluded localized efforts, while logical, also may not stand investigation. Dwyer points out that interstate air pollution was not the initial concern of the 1970 Clean Air Act that focused more on local, intrastate pollution.[14] Accordingly, centralization via national prescriptive controls under the Clean Air Act is not obviously explained by its efficiencies or the failure of localities to adopt improved standards of air quality. Other motives in the political process linked to rent-seeking seem a plausible alternative explanation. Indeed, in light of documented quality of life improvements with lower air pollution, it is possible that decentralized Coasean exchange would have been a workable option. With local efforts, transaction costs would have been lower, information greater, and incentives apparent for a weighing of the tradeoffs of reduced emissions with costly shifts in manufacturing production, consumption, and automobile transit. Where possible, decentralized decisions might have been more equitable and better balanced marginal social costs and benefits. Unfortunately, these decentralized decisions were precluded by the overarching prescriptions of the Clean Air Act. The chapter addresses how that took place, the role of rent-seeking, and the nature of the costs generated.

## 4.2 LEGISLATIVE HISTORY OF THE CLEAN AIR ACT AND THE ADOPTION OF CENTRALIZED POLLUTION CONTROL

As detailed by Stern, McCubbins et al., Dwyer, Orford, and Daniels et al., the political process in the design and administration of the Clean Air Act amendments was a complicated one, involving lobbyists, the courts, and differently motivated members of the House, the Senate, and the President.[15] There were distinct objectives driven

---

[14] Dwyer, The practice of federalism under the Clean Air Act, 1220, argues that interstate pollution controls under Clean Air Act amendments did not receive attention until 1977, with major provisions being made in the 1990 Amendments.

[15] Stern, A. C. (1982). History of air pollution legislation in the United States. *Journal of the Air Pollution Control Association*, 32 (1): 44–61; McCubbins et al., Political

## 4.2 LEGISLATIVE HISTORY OF THE CLEAN AIR ACT

by philosophical, health, economic, and reelection concerns.[16] The legislative history reveals considerable debate and over time, political impasse. The disputes generally were not over the efficient provision of a public good, improved air quality across a heterogeneous country, but rather over the federal law's extent, the distribution of regulation, compliance, and limiting interregional competition over air quality and industrial activity. Transaction cost reduction as described by Coase, does not arise in the debates as prominent drivers of the legislation. Rent-seeking through raising rivals' costs, limiting entry, and securing privately desired environmental qualities at low direct cost to some recipients provides a compelling explanation for the provisions of the Clean Air Act.

Law reviews and other professional journal articles are useful for understanding the Clean Air Act of 1963, the Amendments of 1970, 1977, and 1990, and how a centralized regulatory structure came to be instead of economic property rights and decentralized Coasean exchange. To begin, Stern lists and evaluates major federal air pollution control legislation from 1955 through 1977. Although Stern provides no clear evaluation baseline, he views air pollution accomplishments prior to 1970 as limited.[17] Orford also outlines federal air pollution mitigation legislation prior to 1970. He describes the origins of the Clean Air Act of 1963 as setting the basis for the more powerful 1970 Clean Air Act Amendments.[18]

In Orford's thorough description of background for the laws, drawing from the secondary literature and some agency and

---

control of agencies; Dwyer, The practice of federalism under the Clean Air Act; Orford, The Clean Air Act of 1963; and Daniels, B., Follett, J. P., and Davis, J. (2020). The making of the Clean Air Act. *Hastings Law Journal*, 71 (4). Article 3: 901. https://repository.uchastings.edu/hastings_law_journal/vol71/iss4/3.

[16] Discussion of lobbying and exchanges with politicians is in Bombardini, M., and Trebbi, F. (2020). Empirical models of lobbying. *Annual Review of Economics*, 12: 391–413. See also, Aces, A. (2024). Influence seeking in the federal bureaucracy: Do groups lobby or monitor policymakers? *Quarterly Journal of Political Science*, 19 (1): 27–52.

[17] Stern, History of air pollution legislation in the United States.

[18] Orford, The Clean Air Act of 1963.

congressional reports, there emerges a basic philosophical call by key advocates – some politicians, academic and media observers, and environmental lobby group representatives for "harnessing that massive regulatory potential [*of the federal government*] to improve U.S. society."[19] He points to a legacy of federal efforts in the New Deal to devise industrial policies for confronting the Great Depression as a template for federal government intervention on environmental issues.[20] The notion of marshalling the power of the federal government to advance society, associated with the New Deal and Civil Rights legislation, appears to have been important for political lobby advocates in moving their desired Clean Air Act provisions forward.[21] Such efforts stressed the benefits of their proposals and not a weighing of relative costs and benefits or of determining who would bear any differential consequences.

Orford also asserts that the US government took regulatory control in 1963 "because the alternative – fragmentary local control – was not working. The first solution, to maintain a cooperative state-federal abatement program largely in control of state decisionmakers, also did not work." With enactment of the 1963 Clean Air Act, "it was possible for Congress to enact more robust federal enforcement powers in 1970." Senator Edmund Muskie of Maine, a floor leader for the Clean Air Act Amendments of 1970 concluded: "state and local governments have not responded adequately to this challenge. It is clear that enforcement must be toughened if we are to meet the national deadlines. More tools are needed, and the Federal presence and backup authority must be increased."[22]

---

[19] Orford, The Clean Air Act of 1963, 12, bracketed italicized insertion added; see also 16, 29–57.

[20] The impact of the New Deal, however, is far more nuanced, complex, and in some cases, limited than Orford suggests. See Fishback, P. (2017). How successful was the new deal? The microeconomic impact of New Deal spending and lending policies in the 1930s. *Journal of Economic Literature*, 55 (4): 1–51; Fishback, P., and Kachanovskaya, V. (2015). The multiplier for federal spending in the states during the Great Depression. *Journal of Economic History*, 75 (1): 125–162.

[21] Dwyer, The practice of federalism under the Clean Air Act, 1224.

[22] Dwyer, The practice of federalism under the Clean Air Act, 1191 n. 32.

There is no empirical basis in this literature for concluding that local, cooperative arrangements were ineffective or "did not work." Conclusions were based upon hypothetical standards that were assumed by political proponents to be beneficial relative to the status quo. If local parties were more measured in their approach to air quality improvements, that may have reflected consideration of area costs and a balancing of gains and losses. Such localized weighing was not feasible under federal air pollution control mandates. Identifying ways of promoting local and regional air pollution reductions in lieu of federal intervention could have been an option, but as with other federal environmental legislation examined in this volume, that was not the aim. Indeed, even if there might have been local pathways, given the determination of proponents and their strong normative beliefs that federalization was the optimal abatement mechanism, it is not obvious that even compelling successful city and state alternative efforts might have carried the day.

According to Orford, with rising per capita incomes, greater urbanization, and more information from the Public Health Service on the negative health effects of air pollution, especially from particulates, Nitrogen Oxides ($NO_x$), $SO_2$, and carbon monoxide ($CO$), there was an emerging political imperative held by some for confronting air pollution in urban areas. Environmental lobby groups coalesced around the issue. As previously noted, voluntary, localized efforts in the 1960s to address air pollution, such as in Pittsburgh and St. Louis, were viewed by advocates for more federal intervention along with some members of Congress as being too disconnected, slow, and unenforced.

Orford's appraisal of the Clean Air Act's (CAA) legislative history reveals that imposed costs and tradeoffs played little role in congressional determination of what uniform federal air pollution standards might accomplish under the 1963 Clean Air Act and its subsequent amendments. Orford portrays the debate in Congress between proponents and opponents as largely driven by ideological assessments of the way to move forward on air pollution control at the federal level where some anti-statists Republicans competed with New Deal progressive Democrats. Even so, the Clean Air Act of 1963 (Pub. L. 88-206, 77 Stat.392) passed 273–102 in the House and 89–11 in the Senate.

Daniels et al. describe the political origins of the Clean Air Act of 1970 by following the positions and interactions among the President, key Senators and House members, Executive Office officials, EPA Directors and staff, as well as representatives of the American automobile industry, National Association of Manufacturers, and environmental NGOs, including the Sierra Club, Natural Resources Defense Council, and Environmental Defense Fund.[23] The authors point to the political attraction of addressing growing environmental concerns, considering the divisive political conditions that existed in 1970 with opposition to the Viet Nam war, inflation, and an economic recession.[24] The 1962 publication of *Silent Spring* by Rachel Carson and the 1969 Santa Barbara oil spill galvanized environmental organizations, especially among students. It was followed by the 1970 first Earth Day, promoted by Senator Gaylord Nelson of Wisconsin, to direct attention to environmental degradation. The powerful rise of the conservation movement as a social and political force is described by Coglianese.[25]

As argued by Orford, existing air pollution legislation had not defined wide ranging federal government involvement in addressing air pollution.[26] The 1970, 1977, and 1990 Clean Air Act Amendments, however, did so, and the question is why? Was this shift due to high transaction costs that precluded effective local and interregional controls or was it driven more by pecuniary and nonpecuniary, philosophical rent-seeking? Once the Clean Air Act of 1970 was enacted and the EPA was authorized to draft and implement

---

[23] Daniels et al., The making of the Clean Air Act, 901, 903–906.
[24] Daniels et al., The making of the Clean Air Act, 903, claim broad popular appeal of environmental issues, but this claim is not documented. Given a large and heterogeneous population and inherent collective action problems, it seems likely that more well-organized environmental groups voiced concerns and lobbied members of Congress and the President.
[25] Coglianese, Social movements, law, and society.
[26] Orford, The Clean Air Act of 1963. 1955 Air Pollution Control Act, Pub. L. No. 159-360, 69 Stat 322; 1963 Clean Air Act, Pub. L. No. 88-206, 77 Stat. 392; 1965 Motor Vehicle Pollution Control Act, Pub. L. No. 89-272, 79 Stat. 992.

its authorized regulatory programs, the EPA staff apparently became another element in nonpecuniary rent-seeking. Although there were different views among the politicians regarding costs and benefits and their political ramifications, EPA officials, who did not bear those costs, appear to have become ideologically aligned with imposing national ambient air quality standards, enforcing deadlines in meeting them, and requiring State Implementation Plans (SIP) to implement national mandates. EPA staff were described in the *Wall Street Journal* as generally "young, enthusiastic environmentalists with ideological commitment to the mission of the agency."[27]

Cost issues were raised in congressional debates between Senate advocates and more cautious members of the House and the President. The chief proponent of the emerging legislation, Muskie, is said to have "challenged his colleagues in committee, on the floor, and in conference to defend anything less than *forcing technology to achieve healthy air by a date standard*. None did." Directed innovation forced the automobile industry, steel mills, pulp and petrochemicals, and utilities, the major sources of air pollution, to meet required emissions reductions by EPA deadlines.[28] Achievement of the standards was the objective. Industry was to come up with ways of implementing pollution controls within the fixed timelines via forced, directed innovation.

National standards, deadlines for achieving a 90 percent reduction in hydrocarbons and carbon monoxide, and the role of technology-forcing in meeting them, were debated in the Senate as the 1970 law was being drafted. Citizen court suits were invited in the Senate, later incorporated in administration of the law under the notion of the Public Trust Doctrine (PTD) to force compliance with the law's deadlines.[29]

---

[27] Daniels et al., The making of the Clean Air Act, 901, 937, 956.
[28] Daniels et al., The making of the Clean Air Act, 927.
[29] Daniels et al., The making of the Clean Air Act, 901, 931–932. The Clean Air Act allows citizens to file lawsuits against those who violate emission standards or limitations, or orders issued by the EPA or a state. This includes the ability to sue the EPA Administrator for failing to perform their duties under the Clean Air Act.

The attraction of citizen suits for Clean Air Act advocates, then and today, was that they suggested popular support for the legislation and generated political pressure for adhering to EPA regulations. Citizen suits, however, may not reflect broad-based citizen positions, as compared to those of more organized, politically active, urban, wealthier, and more highly educated segments of the population. While collective action challenges are apt to be too great to reach a general population consensus and lead to representative citizen suits as suggested by advocates, they can be a source of rent-seeking for more narrowly focused groups in advertising their objectives as being broadly popular.[30]

Indeed, the courts became a driver in Clean Air Act implementation. Environmental NGOs such as Natural Resources Defense Council, Sierra Club, National Wildlife Federation, and Environmental Defense Fund were active in the process.[31] They challenged EPA delays in meeting transportation emission control targets as well as the agency's granting states extensions in implementing the national ambient air quality standards. The costs of the back and forth among environmental and industry litigants, the states, and the EPA as detailed in the legislative histories might exceed any possible transaction costs associated with decentralized, negotiated pollution controls.

The Clean Air Act of 1970 (42 U.S.C. §7401 et seq.) and its amendments of 1977 and 1990 outline the principal air quality laws for the US and possibly are the most significant US environmental statutes.[32]

---

[30] Aldy et al., Looking back at 50 years of the Clean Air Act, 179, point out that the Clean Air Act empowered citizens with the right to sue government officials as well as regulated entities that failed to perform their duties. For discussion of the issues involved in interpreting poll data, see Berinsky, Measuring public opinion with surveys.

[31] Aldy, et al. Looking back at 50 years of the Clean Air Act. Daniels et al., The making of the Clean Air Act, 901, 952–953. See, for example, *Delaney* v. *EPA*, 898 F.2d 687, 691 (9th Cir. 1990). David S. Baron, Arizona Center for Law in the Public Interest, Tucson, Ariz., for petitioners. The Arizona Center for Law in the Public Interest is an environmental advocacy organization.

[32] Van Doren, P., and Firey, T. A. (2017). Regulation at 40, March 22. 34–36. https://ssrn.com/abstract=2974225 or http://dx.doi.org/10.2139/ssrn.2974225.

In their review of the economics of the Clean Air Act, Currie and Walker state that the law "is one of the most far-reaching pieces of regulatory legislation ever passed in the United States.[33] Arguably, it affects just about all aspects of daily life, either directly through the air we breathe and the cars we drive or indirectly by altering prices and the location of jobs and industries." The authors point out that the 1970 Clean Air Act relied exclusively on command-and-control regulations for reducing air pollution and generating health benefits with those public goods objectives generally outweighing consideration of potential economic costs or the alternative of decentralized pollution control.[34]

## 4.3 PROVISIONS OF THE 1963 CLEAN AIR ACT AMENDMENTS OF 1970, 1977, 1990

The Clean Air Act amendments addresses nationwide air pollution via NAAQS, State Implementation Plans (SIPs), New Source Performance Standards (NSPS), and National Emission Standards for Hazardous Air Pollutants. Key pollutants are CO, lead (Pb), particulate matter (PM), ozone ($O_3$), nitrogen dioxide ($NO_2$), and $SO_2$.

Amendments to the 1963 Clean Air Act in 1970, 1977, and 1990, along with judicial rulings, authorized the EPA to set uniform national ambient air quality standards (quantities) and to regulate emissions for stationary, mobile, old, and new sources of hazardous air pollutants. It did not rely upon Pigouvian taxes (prices).[35] States were to draft SIPs to meet the standards by December 31, 1975. Counties that met or exceeded them were deemed to be in attainment, and counties that did not meet them were deemed to be in nonattainment. Under the Prevention of Significant Air Quality Deterioration (PSD) and New Source Emission Review restrictions added with the 1977 amendments, air quality above the NAAQS in

---

[33] Currie and Walker, What do economists have to say about the Clean Air Act, 21–22.
[34] Currie and Walker, What do economists have to say about the Clean Air Act, 5–6.
[35] Clean Air Act of 1963, Pub. L. 88-206, 77 Stat. 392 (1963).

attainment counties was not to be compromised by new sources of pollution, even if they posed no threat to ambient standards.[36]

Prevention of Significant Deterioration (PSD) of Air Quality Standards under the Clean Air Act applied to all attainment and nonattainment areas.[37] Initially promulgated in the early 1970s by the EPA and formalized with the Clean Air Act Amendments of 1977, PSD rules were designed to reduce particulates, $SO_2$, and $NO_x$ emissions, primarily from coal-fired power plants and industrial firms. The issue was whether the PSD mandated air qualities were to be applied to attainment regions where air qualities were already above national standards or just to nonattainment areas. A broad application of PSD was strongly supported by environmental organizations. When the EPA initially determined that Congress had not intended to impose PSD restrictions on regions with high air quality, the Sierra Club successfully sued, and the Supreme Court held that Prevention of Significant Deterioration applied to attainment counties as well.[38] Moreover as explored below, firms and unions located in nonattainment areas, along with their political representatives had rent-seeking reasons to back broad application of PSD.

The 1977 amendments also introduced New Source Emission Review, regulating new or modified sources of pollution in attainment counties that had not previously faced as much regulatory scrutiny.[39] Along with Prevention of Significant Deterioration, New Source Emission Review required that new or modified plants in attainment counties were to adopt the best available control technologies to hold air quality at existing high levels. In nonattainment counties, new or modified stationary sources of air pollution were

---

[36] Maloney, M. T., and McCormick, R. E. (1982). A positive theory of environmental quality regulation. *Journal of Law and Economics*, 25 (1): 99–123, 118–119.

[37] Revesz, Federalism and environmental regulation, 576.

[38] *Sierra Club* v. *Ruckelshaus*, 344 F. Supp. 253 (D.D.C. 1972), aff'd per curiam by an equally divided Court sub nom. *Fri* v. *Sierra Club*, 412 U.S. 541 (1973). See McCubbins et al., Political control of agencies, 452–453.

[39] Nonattainment New Source Review applies to nonattainment regions.

required to adopt technologies with the lowest achievable emission rate and to offset emissions through acquisition of reductions by another facility. Markets emerged for offsets.[40]

Counties deemed to be nonattainment were to be evaluated annually by the EPA as to progress in meeting the standards. Failure of states to draft plans for reaching attainment would lead the agency to withhold a variety of federal funding sources for land use and transport, to ban permits for construction of plants that might generate new sources of pollutants, and to impose its own plan for attainment.[41] Industry specific emissions standards for pollution sources were set, and affected facilities in nonattainment counties were required to adopt the lowest achievable emissions rate technologies. As part of its authority over mobile sources, the EPA regulated most motor vehicles, wielding the power to impose testing and certification requirements for engines and to require designated fuel formulations and additives.

Plants in nonattainment counties were regulated more strictly than those in attainment counties. PSD rules for attainment counties, however, meant that firms could not easily relocate to them. Mobility might have been a lower economic cost method of meeting the national standards. Firm migration and restructuring might have included new capital investment and other refinements that reduced emissions, made economically feasible by less stringent regulation in attainment counties. The NSE, however, raised the costs of firm migration and enforced Clean Air Act uniform quality mandates on areas with relatively cleaner air. Citizens in those settings could not compromise existing air quality by inviting the migration of some new industrial plants and employment.

Under the Clean Air Act, national air pollution targets or quality standards were set by the EPA, based upon epidemiological and

---

[40] Shapiro, J. S., and Walker, R. (2004). Is air pollution regulation too lenient? Evidence from US offset markets. *NBER Working Paper*, No. 28199, 2020, revised 2024. National Bureau of Economic Research.

[41] Dwyer, The practice of federalism under the Clean Air Act, 1193.

integrated-assessment model estimates. Regulated firms and other private actors were required to adjust to them. There were no requirements for ex ante analyses of incremental benefits from gradual air quality standard adjustments relative to additional costs nor were there apparent in-depth ex ante examination of who bore the costs or received benefits in setting the targets across the country.

Regulatory Impact Analysis (RIA) was added in 1981, eleven years after the 1970 Clean Air Act by Presidential Executive Order calling for examination of the effects of proposed policies that might have an estimated annual impact of $100 million or more.[42] Carey describes how the use and focus of RIAs has varied across Presidential Administrations since then.[43] This suggests both an overarching emphasis on pollution reduction relative to costs, as well as the potential for rents to be achieved by agents in the way in which the Clean Air Act is administered.[44] Otherwise, why would such studies come so late and be controversial?

The law granted sweeping powers to the EPA to require specific air pollution mitigation measures and timelines. Significant moderation was not negotiable across the many sectors affected nationwide. Dwyer describes the EPA's powers: "This astonishingly open-ended provision [of the 1970 law] not only gave EPA enormous authority to intrude directly into a policy-making area that states had historically controlled, it also effectively required EPA to do so."[45]

Dwyer also recognized the diversity of conditions in the US where uniform standards were perpetrated:

> The Nation spans a continent, with an astonishing range of environmental conditions and problems.[46] Differences in

---

[42] Aldy et al., Looking back at 50 years of the Clean Air Act, 185.
[43] Carey, M. P. (2011). Federal rulemaking: The role of the Office of Information and Regulatory Affairs. Congressional Research Service. https://crsreports.congress.govRL32397s.
[44] Carey, Federal rulemaking.
[45] Dwyer, The practice of federalism under the Clean Air Act, 1201.
[46] Dwyer, The practice of federalism under the Clean Air Act, 1218.

climate and weather (e.g., patterns of temperature, wind, rainfall, humidity), geography (e.g., deserts, mountains, plains, coastal regions), the relative importance of sources and types of pollution (e.g., cars, large utilities and factories, numerous small sources), environmental and public health risks (e.g., special need for visibility control, size of affected human population), and economic conditions confound attempts to have a successful, highly centralized regulatory program.[47]

Over time, the Clean Air Act's complexities and range seemingly have grown beyond what was negotiated in Congress in 1970, where despite Coase's 1960 paper, economists apparently played little role.[48] Schmalensee and Stavins note: "This law, only twenty-four pages in length, gave the EPA considerable discretion and authority to set and change regulations and to enforce compliance."[49]

Daniels et al. indicate that there was some recognition of the differential costs and benefits of the National Ambient Air Quality Standards and the related No Significant Deterioration of air quality across rich and poor counties. In terms of the federal Clean Water Act with its prescribed controls, the Governor of Alabama, one of the nation's poorest states, apparently advertised in Indiana papers with a statement quoted by EPA Director Ruckelshaus: "'Bring your industry down here. It is okay with us if you pour some stuff in the river. We want jobs.'"[50]

Federally imposed uniform standards and compliance mandates were promoted by political advocates as being necessary to avoid a race to the bottom by states and localities that would undermine national air quality objectives.[51] For example, Senator Prouty of Vermont claimed: "To be sure, minimum Federal standards are a

---

[47] Dwyer, The practice of federalism under the Clean Air Act, 1195.
[48] Schmalensee and Stavins, Policy evolution under the Clean Air Act, 28.
[49] Schmalensee and Stavins, Policy evolution under the Clean Air Act, 28.
[50] Daniels et al., The making of the Clean Air Act, 924.
[51] Dwyer, The practice of federalism under the Clean Air Act, 1195.

must, as they free the 50 States from the necessity of competing for business by lowering their standards."[52]

Although the rhetorical logic of the race-to-the-bottom argument is clear, there seems to be no empirical analysis of the conditions under which agents (or in this case, governments) would compete to fully dissipate programmatic (air quality) benefits or rents. Or if they did compete, that the process would have reduced local or aggregate well-being on net. The argument is analogous to an open-access resource where competitors for asset values, such as a fishery, fully commit and competitively waste the resource with incumbent social and economic losses.[53] Complete dissipation, however, requires that the parties be homogeneous in costs and objectives. In light of the vast variation in economic conditions across the country, including incomes, employment opportunities, as well as air pollution costs, it seems clear that states and regions were not homogenous.

The costs and benefits of air pollution controls would have varied dramatically, and desired levels of air pollution would have differed. These factors would have influenced competition among the states. Not all would have participated. There would not have been a uniform "bottom" for local governments to race to.[54] With plant migration air quality in initial regions would have improved as older, polluting plants were decommissioned and air quality in receiving regions reduced as new economic activity, perhaps with new technologies took place. It might have all been pareto improving.

## 4.4 COSTS OF THE CLEAN AIR ACT

Daniels et al. describe political lobbying over the Clean Air Act's potential costs on specific industries, usually coal burning or energy

---

[52] Dwyer, The practice of federalism under the Clean Air Act, 1195 n. 60.
[53] Gordon, The economic theory of a common-property resource.
[54] A race-to-the-bottom argument as justification for central federal regulation is challenged by Revesz, R. L. (1992). Rehabilitating interstate competition: Rethinking the "race to the bottom" rationale for federal environmental regulation. *New York University Law Review*, 67: 1210–1254.

intensive, and the industrial Northeast and Midwest.[55] The Ford administration in 1974 pushed unsuccessfully for rollbacks on the Clean Air Act. The Reagan administration in 1981 also resisted the full enforcement of the law. Politicians representing regions with steel mills, coal producing operations, and auto industries sought adjustments, but were countered by consortiums of environmental groups who lobbied Congressional supporters.[56] Similarly, Senator Byrd of West Virginia added a provision to the 1990 Clean Air Act amendments for $500 million to cover lost salaries for mine workers put out of work. The provision lost 49–50 in the Senate.[57]

These political battles were inevitable in a setting where policies were endorsed and advocated within a charged political environment and where there were no tradable instruments to adjust for new cost and benefit information. Benefits and costs are unlikely to be evenly distributed through the political, rent-seeking process, generating winners and losers.[58]

In their review of cost/benefit considerations in the Clean Air Act for the Congressional Research Service, McCarthy and Lattanzio provide lists of Clean Air Act provisions that either mention or imply cost considerations as well as those that do not do so.[59] The authors conclude that about half of the major regulatory programs mention costs or economic considerations explicitly, and others imply that costs may be considered; "but other authorizing sections, including some *key* sections, make no mention of cost considerations" (italics added).[60]

---

[55] Daniels et al., The making of the Clean Air Act, 956.
[56] Reitze, The legislative history of US air pollution control.
[57] Reitze, The legislative history of US air pollution control, 721.
[58] Stigler, G. (1971). The theory of economic regulation. *Bell Journal of Economics and Management Science*, 2 (1): 3–21.
[59] McCarthy and Lattanzio, Cost and benefit considerations. Quote from article summary. The authors list costs that are considered and not considered as well as estimated magnitudes across sectors and states: Clean Air Act Authorizing Provisions That Mention or Imply Consideration of Cost, table 1; table 2. Clean Air Act Authorizing Provisions That Do Not Mention Cost.
[60] McCarthy and Lattanzio, Cost and benefit considerations. Quote from article summary, first bullet point.

In general, regulatory compliance costs have not been critical in setting and implementing the National Ambient Air Quality Standards (NAAQS). Cost issues were raised in 1976 when three coal fired power plants near St. Louis in a nonattainment area, petitioned the DC Circuit Court for relief, arguing that fulfillment was financially impossible. The DC Court and subsequently, the US Supreme Court dismissed requests for assistance based on costs. In *Union Electric v. EPA*, 427 US 246 (1976), the Supreme Court ruled that economic and technological infeasibility claims could not be considered in challenging State Implementation Plans (SIP) approved by the EPA. Costs were not in the agency's approval criteria under the Clean Air Act. The Court's rationale was that Congress had intended strict compliance with the NAAQS, forcing industries to adopt pollution control technologies. The EPA's role was to consider whether the SIPs met statutory criteria, which did not include economic or technical feasibility.[61]

In 1997, the EPA revised upwards the NAAQS for particulates and $O_3$, and the American Trucking Associations, Inc., other private organizations, as well as the States of Michigan, Ohio, and West Virginia challenged the new standards. In *Whitman v. American Trucking*, 531 US 457 2001, the Supreme Court held that while the EPA had discretion in setting and implementing standards, it could not consider financial effects in doing so. The EPA was to assess whether or not SIPs met the NAAQS and not to define how the SIPs were to meet them.[62]

In another case, however, the EPA was directed to consider costs in deciding to regulate specific facilities. Regulation of mercury and arsenic emissions from certain coal- and oil-fired steam-generating

---

[61] The Supreme Court held that "Congress intended claims of economic and technological infeasibility to be wholly foreign to the Administrator's consideration of a state implementation plan" (*Union Elec. Co.*, 427 U.S. at 256). Quoted in Daniels et al., The making of the Clean Air Act, 957).

[62] The US Supreme Court ruled in 2001 in *Whitman v. American Trucking Associations Inc* (531 U.S. 457), that the Clean Air Act "unambiguously bars cost considerations from the [pollution limits]-setting process." States had considerable flexibility in defining how they met the NAAQS and the instruments used in doing so.

power plants under the 1990 Clean Air Act Amendments and the EPA's Air Toxic Rule was estimated to cost $9.6 billion per year. In 2000, the EPA determined that costs should not be considered in promulgating regulations if they were considered appropriate and necessary. Cost considerations were reserved for later in the regulatory process. A group of nonprofit organizations, corporations, and twenty-three states challenged EPA's conclusion. The US Circuit Court for the District of Columbia upheld the EPA in 2014, but upon appeal, the US Supreme Court reversed the decision. In *Michigan v. Environmental Protection Agency*, 576 U.S. 743 (2015) the court ruled that the EPA went beyond its delegated authority.[63] The agency was to consider costs and benefits in determining whether the power plant regulation was appropriate and necessary, not after the regulatory decision was made.

Beyond judicial rulings on Clean Air Act costs, Greenstone finds that during 1972–1987, nonattainment counties, where regulations were most binding, lost approximately 590,000 jobs, $37 billion in capital stock, and $75 billion of output in pollution-intensive industries (1987 USD).[64] Currie and Walker point out that if a worker is unemployed for long periods of time and/or cannot find a comparable paying job in future years, the uncompensated transitional costs of finding new employment and in reallocating production may be large.[65] Walker investigates the transitional costs of the 1990 Clean Air Act amendments for manufacturing workers due to a change in county-level attainment status.[66] He finds that workers in newly regulated plants lost $5.4 billion (in 1990 USD) in earnings due to the amendments and that these costs were mostly accounted for

---

[63] *Michigan, et al.* v. *EPA*, U.S. Circuit Court of Appeals for the D.C. Circuit, No 14-46 (04-15-2014).
[64] Greenstone, M. (2002). The impacts of environmental regulations on industrial activity: Evidence from the 1970 and 1977 Clean Air Act Amendments and the Census of Manufactures. *Journal of Political Economy*, 110 (6): 1175–1219.
[65] Currie and Walker, What do economists have to say about the Clean Air Act, 15.
[66] Walker, R. (2013). The transitional costs of sectoral reallocation: Evidence from the Clean Air Act and the workforce. *Quarterly Journal of Economics*, 128 (4): 1787–1835.

by a combination of delay in finding a new job elsewhere and lower earnings in future positions.[67] The estimated losses for the average worker were equal to 20 percent of annual pre-regulatory earnings.[68]

Greenstone, List, and Syverson examine the effects of the Clean Air Act on manufacturing total factor productivity of polluting establishments in nonattainment counties, where regulations were stricter, relative to similar firms in attainment counties. Their estimated loss of total factor productivity in nonattainment counties corresponds to an annual economic cost of roughly $21 billion, or about 9 percent of manufacturing sector profits between 1972 and 1993.[69]

The analysis of Shapiro and Walker suggests that the costs of additional pollution releases under the Clean Air Act Amendments of 1977 may have been less than the estimated benefits of higher air quality.[70] The law required that new or expanding plants in nonattainment areas purchase pollution-reduction offsets from existing facilities so that overall air quality was not compromised. They find that offset prices were less than the estimated benefits of improved air quality across areas of the country covered, except in Houston, the country's major petrochemical center. Firm expansion and additional employment and production levels that did not take place in light of offset requirements, however, are missing in the cost estimates. These opportunity costs of foregone and hence, unobserved economic activities would be relevant if the standards underlying the offset requirements were too restrictive.

The careful study of Clay et al., is suggestive of the costs of adaptation to emissions regulations.[71] They examine fossil-fuel

---

[67] Currie and Walker, What do economists have to say about the Clean Air Act, 15–16; Walker, The transitional costs of sectoral reallocation.

[68] The transition costs on displaced workers are also addressed by Autor, D., Dorn, D., Hanson, G., and Song, J. (2013). Trade Adjustment: Worker Level Evidence. *NBER Working Paper*, 19226. National Bureau of Economic Research.

[69] Greenstone, M., List, J. A., and Syverson, C. (2012). The effects of environmental regulation on the competitiveness of U.S. Manufacturing. *NBER Working Paper*, No. 18392. National Bureau of Economic Research.

[70] Shapiro and Walker, Is air pollution regulation too lenient?

[71] Clay et al., Impacts of the Clean Air Act on the power sector.

power plants in the United States that dated from 1938–1994 and the impact of EPA regulations after 1970 on production costs and productivity. They find that new technology requirements resulted in a fall in power-plant productivity by 16 percent. Costs were greatest for older vintage plants, where productivity losses ranged from 38 to 58 percent. These plants had fewer options for adjustment, and firm compliance costs could be reduced only by a shifting of production from older to newer plants. With reallocation of power generation from coal plants, annual total productivity losses were about $2.3 billion (2020 USD). In other situations, such as with some heavy industrial facilities, however, a shift to new plants might not have been profitable so that operations closed, and employees had to seek alternatives elsewhere. Search and matching employment shifts were costly, particularly affecting those population segments least able to smoothly respond, a factor that does not seem to have attracted enough attention in assessments of the Clean Air Act.[72]

The distribution of costs and benefits under the Clean Air Act raise environmental justice concerns. Primarily, environmental justice has centered on air pollution hot spots where concentrations of pollutants disproportionately affect underserved, underrepresented populations of low socioeconomic status. Revesz is critical of the EPA's response in addressing these concerns.[73] Even so, if the pollutants primarily are local, then decentralized approaches might have been more flexible and responsive. Property rights in the right to pollute or to be free of pollution could exist and be traded as mitigation.[74] If pollutants also come from transboundary sources, then there are more reasons for federal assistance of some type to promote

---

[72] Kuhn, A., Lalive, R., and Zweimüller, J. (2009). The public health costs of job loss. *Journal of Health Economics*, 28: 1099–1115.

[73] Revesz, R. L. (2022). Air pollution and environmental justice. *Ecology Law Quarterly*, 49: 187–252.

[74] Nash, J. R., and Revesz, R. L. (2001). Markets and geography: Designing marketable permit schemes to control local and regional pollutants. *Ecological Law Quarterly*, 28: 572–574, suggest how hot spot concentrations might be better addressed within the NAAQS.

abatement. These conditions do not necessarily justify centralized regulation, but rather suggest that state, regional, and federal governments might provide frameworks for coordinated responses.

Less advertised environmental justice issues also arise in nonattainment areas where there have been plant closing and uncompensated employment losses. In attainment areas there may be fewer economic opportunities imposed on relevant populations due to restrictions from both Prevention of Significant Deterioration and New Source Emission Review requirements.

## 4.5 EVIDENCE OF RENT-SEEKING: RESTRICTING ENTRY, RAISING RIVALS' COSTS AND SECURING PARTICULARISTIC, STRONGLY HELD GOALS VIA CLEAN AIR ACT PROVISIONS

The question arises, who might have sought Prevention of Significant Deterioration (PSD) and New Source Review restrictions on firm migration and new plant investment and why? Rent-seeking through raising rival's costs and limiting entry could be an approach taken by certain industry representatives and their political sponsors.[75] One study by Maloney and McCormick tests the raising rivals' costs hypothesis.[76] They examine changes in the profitability of established smelting firms in nonattainment regions after judicial rulings assigned PSD rules to attainment regions and plants within them. The rulings potentially raised the costs for competitive entry by new smelters in those areas. Such barriers had not existed previously. Maloney and McCormick statistically follow market returns for incumbent firms listed on the NYSE around a window of key US District court rulings prior to a 1974 US Supreme Court affirmation of PSD regulation.[77] They find positive profitability shifts for listed polluting firms,

---

[75] Revesz, Federalism and environmental regulation, 575–577.
[76] Maloney and McCormick, A positive theory of environmental quality regulation, 118–119.
[77] District and Appeals Court cases are described briefly in Maloney and McCormick, A positive theory of environmental quality regulation, 118; *Fri* v. *Sierra Club*, 412 US 541, 1973.

consistent with a profitable, rent-seeking hypothesis.[78] Nash and Revesz also describe how New Source Performance Standards (NSPS), New Source Review, and Prevention of Significant Deterioration requirements under the Clean Air Act Amendments of 1970 and 1977 served to grandfather benefits for incumbent firms and to inflict costs on potential new competitors.[79] They argue that rules served to prolong the existence of older, dirtier facilities and distorted investment decisions to avoid stringent New Source Emission Reviews.

Congressional voting patterns on the 1977 amendments are also consistent with rent-seeking efforts to impose PSD costs on regions where economic activity might move. These differential voting patterns are documented by Pashigian and McCubbins et al.[80] Members of Congress from more urban, industrial Northeastern, Mid-Atlantic, and New England states voted for Prevention of Significant Deterioration restrictions and those from more rural southern and western states where industry might move voted against.

Another form of rent-seeking arises when advocates for maintaining high air quality in attainment areas secure their nonpecuniary preferences without having to bear much direct cost. For example, in opposition to marketable permit schemes under the Clean Air Act, a representative of the Natural Resources Defense Council and the National Clean Air Coalition asserted that: "The pristine air quality in the West is a global treasure."[81] The notion was that the relocation of dirty plants to those areas should not be facilitated by the ability

---

[78] McCubbins et al., Political control of agencies, 452–453. See also Revesz, Federalism and environmental regulation, 575–577, for similar rent-seeking arguments as motivation for PSD.

[79] Nash, J. R., and Revesz, R. L. (2007). Grandfathering and environmental regulation: The law and economics of new source review. *Northwestern University Law Review*, 101 (4): 1677–1733, 1681–1696, 1707–1720, for detailed analysis of the use of grandfathering and rent-seeking in the New Source Review provision in the administration of the Clean Air Act.

[80] Pashigian, B. P. (1985). Environmental regulation: Whose self-interests are being protected? *Economic Inquiry*, 23 (4): 551–574; McCubbins et al., Political control of agencies. See also Buchanan and Tullock, Polluters' profits and political response, 139–147.

[81] Nash and Revesz, Markets and geography, 591.

to purchase offset permits in more polluted regions and to transfer production and emissions to the West. While this private value is understandable, it potentially imposed nonnegotiable constraints on populations living in areas with pristine air. Under the Clean Air Act, their preferences would only be considered through adjustments within the political process, and not through market negotiations.

## 4.6 INCENTIVE-BASED INSTRUMENTS WITHIN THE CLEAN AIR ACT

This section does not provide a complete review of the limited and late use of incentive-based instruments within the Clean Air Act. A review is provided by Aldy et al.[82] Such instruments are within the prescriptive caps of the legislation but involve the assignment and trade of use rights or the right to pollute within it. Keohane et al. note that the use of incentive instruments within policy standards is relatively rare, and they suggest rent-seeking as an explanation for this pattern.[83]

Incentive-based systems use tradable rights to pollute, giving firms an incentive to select low-cost abatement, banking unused permits, or trading them. Depending on the design of the program, cap-and-trade makes regulated entities residual claimants to mitigation efficiencies within the preset cap. These instruments are found for instance in Acid Rain regulation, the US Lead Phaseout in fuels, RECLAIM in the Los Angeles Basin, greenhouse gas emission reduction in California, as well as in fisheries with the adoption of individual transferable quotas, as described in Chapter 5. All programs tended to be implemented late in the overall regulatory process, clustering after 1990. Stavins argues that the 1990 shift to market-based instruments in the Clean Air Act was driven by support from the President, members of Congress, agency officials in the EPA, and certain environmental NGOs, such as Environmental Defense Fund (EDF) because of their efficiency potentials.[84]

---

[82] Aldy et al., Looking back at 50 years of the Clean Air Act, 187–211.
[83] Keohane et al., The choice of regulatory instruments, 315.
[84] Stavins, R. N. (1998). What can we learn from the grand policy experiment? Lessons from SO2 allowance trading. *Journal of Economic Perspectives*, 12 (3): 69–88.

## 4.6 INCENTIVE-BASED INSTRUMENTS 91

The cap-and-trade system for national acid rain control was added under the 1990 Clean Air Act amendments.[85] These were adopted thirty years after Coase and twenty years after the 1970 Clean Air Act amendments. Actual implementation did not take place until 1995.[86] Nash and Revesz describe the political conflict among politicians in source regions that delayed adoption of restrictions on the interstate transmission of $SO_2$.[87] Concerns primarily were raised by coal-fired electricity-generating facilities and coal-producing regions in the Upper Midwest, West Virginia, and their political supporters over the distribution of control costs.

Within $SO_2$ caps, tradable emission allowances were grandfathered to incumbent coal-fired electricity generating facilities. Grandfathering delivered rents to these units, whose owners would have had to pay for emission permits with auctioning. Across two phases, total $SO_2$ emission goals were met more rapidly and at lower cost than had been forecast.[88]

There can be costly rent-seeking, even when auction is used. MacKenzie summarizes the evolution of pollution auctions.[89] The California air emissions auction and trading program, AB 32, enacted in 2006, authorized tradable pollution permits. As an indication of rent-seeking in the political process, AB 32 has not been the state's only mechanism for addressing greenhouse gases and other pollutants. California has also relied on political mandates to halt internal

---

[85] Schmalensee and Stavins, Policy evolution under the Clean Air Act.
[86] As described by Anderson, T. L., and Libecap, G. D. (2014). *Environmental Markets: A Property Rights Approach*. Cambridge University Press, 159–166, the $SO_2$ allowance market eventually collapsed as various subsequent regulatory interventions to meet a variety of objectives undermined the security and trade of the allowances. See also Schmalensee, R., and Stavins, R. N. (2013). The SO2 allowance trading system: The ironic history of a grand policy experiment. *Journal of Economic Perspectives*, 27 (1): 103–122.
[87] Nash and Revesz, Markets and geography, 584.
[88] Nash and Revesz, Markets and geography, 584–586; and Aldy et al., Looking back at 50 years of the Clean Air Act, 194–195, the $SO_2$ program and RECLAIM. Regional Greenhouse Gas programs are detailed in www.rggi.org/.
[89] MacKenzie, I. A. (2022). The evolution of pollution auctions. *Review of Environmental Economics and Policy*, 16 (1): 1–24.

combustion vehicle sales (cars, trucks, SUVs) in the state by 2035, to restrict natural gas use in homes and businesses, to impose other clean energy regulations, and to require broad disclosure of emissions by all businesses. Nevertheless, the allowance auctions have raised some $3–4 billion annually.

A key efficiency element for auctions is that they be revenue neutral, with revenues returned to taxpayers to reduce distortive taxes.[90] Otherwise a fund becomes attractive for political distribution of rents. Although 35 percent of the Greenhouse Reduction Fund is to benefit lower income residents to make the program more equitable and revenue neutral, much of the rest is directed to politically directed outlays, some of which are to subsidize risky new alternative energy technologies.[91]

The successes of the national $SO_2$ allowance market and a similar, more localized program (RECLAIM) in the Los Angeles Basin to lower $NO_x$ and Sulphur Oxides ($SO_x$) emissions with cap-and-trade permits between 1994 and 2010, meant that property rights and markets could have been the basis for a much broader use of Coasean approaches. Transaction costs were not an inhibiting factor. In the decentralized case, both the cap and the property rights within it would have been defined by decentralized negotiations. As illustration of how much of an anomaly the cap-and-trade program under national $SO_2$ abatement was within the overall prescriptive approach of the Clean Air Act, it has been labeled "the Grand Experiment."[92]

## 4.7 CONCLUSION

The Clean Air Act is prescriptive. It is politically charged with strong advocates and equally strong opponents. No major amendments

---

[90] Hahn, R., and Noll, R. (1982). Designing a market for tradable emissions permits. In Magat, W. A. ed, *Reform of Environmental Regulation*. Brookings. 163–208.
[91] Carl, J., and Fedor, D. (2014). AB 32 cap and trade: An energy policy essay for California's AB 32 cap-and-trade-and-cash back, not cap-and-trade-and-tax. Shultz-Stephenson Task Force on Energy Policy. www.hoover.org/taskforces/energy-policy.
[92] Schmalensee and Stavins, The SO2 allowance trading system.

or legislative revisions have been added since 1990. Although Schmalensee and Stavins assert political polarization is the problem, they do not address the underlying reason for sharp political differences.[93] A primary source of conflict between advocates and opponents is competition over the political rents associated with the law's controls and the disproportionate net costs they impose.

The law levies national ambient air quality standards on a heterogeneous nation where costs and benefits of air pollution abatement certainly would have varied. It also restricts firm and plant mobility as a mechanism for compliance, possibly encouraging investment and movement to other countries. Because the initial focus of the Clean Air Act was on intrastate air pollution where the numbers of parties was limited and more information was available on local tradeoffs, the transaction costs of the alternative of Coasean abatement might not have been prohibitive.

A decentralized Coasean approach might have allowed local or regional negotiations to set air quality standards with parties weighing health and other economic benefits with imposed economic costs. These marginal benefit/cost discussions might have included the effects of proposed air quality restrictions on existing plants, new facilities, and associated employment as well as on overall economic activity, relative to estimated health benefits and other improvements. These factors might have been weighed by communities in determining what air quality standards they desired, not as a reaction to those set exogenously. Control of extensively transmitted pollutants, such as ozone would have required interstate coordination, and the federal government could have played a role in facilitating such efforts. Doing so seemingly did not require the observed elements of the Clean Air Act. A Coasean bargaining framework would have been more open; generated more information on costs and benefits; and left less role for politicians, administrative agencies, and national advocacy groups. Impediments to localized efforts might have been

---

[93] Schmalensee and Stavins, Policy evolution under the Clean Air Act.

addressed in federal legislation with alternative judicial and regulatory actions to lower transaction costs rather than the effective nationalization of air pollution abatement.

To further understand the role of rent-seeking in externality mitigation, two additional empirical cases are provided in detail in Chapters 5 and 6. The first is the Magnuson-Stevens Fishery Act of 1976. The second case is the Endangered Species Act of 1973. As detailed, neither law primarily relies upon Coase's framework, although Magnuson-Stevens ultimately adopted regional management councils and catch shares as limited property rights when its initial input and output controls failed to halt overfishing. In both cases, directed restrictions have had significant costs assigned to specific parties as well as to general society. It is unclear how effective either law is, relative to a baseline where property rights and market exchange were an alternative mechanism to address externalities.

# 5 Rent-Seeking, Economic Property Rights, and Coasean Trade

*US Fisheries Regulation*

> for natural resources-as for other types of wealth-"everybody's property is nobody's property." No one will take the trouble to husband and maintain a resource unless he has a reasonable certainty of receiving some portion of the product of his management; that is, unless he has some property right in the yield.
>
> A. Scott, The fishery.

> For over three decades, the world's marine fish stocks have come under increasing pressure from fishing... there is massive overcapacity in the global fleet. ...The most critical reform is the effective removal of the open access condition from marine capture fisheries and the institution of secure marine tenure and property rights systems.
>
> World Bank et al., *Sunken Billions*.

> The Congress finds and declares ... The fish off the coasts of the United States... constitute valuable and renewable natural resources ... As a consequence of increased fishing pressure and because of the inadequacy of fishery conservation and management practices and controls...certain stocks of such fish have been overfished.... Many coastal areas are dependent upon fishing and related activities, and their economies have been badly damaged by the overfishing... A national program for the conservation and management of the fishery resources of the United States is necessary to prevent overfishing ... [via] a fishery conservation zone within which the United States will assume exclusive fishery management authority ...
>
> Senate Report on the Magnuson-Stevens Act, 16 U.S.C. Title 16.[1]

---

[1] *Senate Report on the Magnuson-Stevens Act* (1976) 16 U.S.C. Title 16, Chapter 38, Sec. 1801.

> Opposition is based on the realization that any form of access control represents a specific allocation of benefits that advantages some participants over others. Thus, the characteristic concern ... on the implications for distributional equity.
>
> S. Macinko, Public or private?[2]
>
> ITQs are the creation of economists ... ITQs reduce the number of boats in the fleet and can increase unemployment ... ITQs typically result in the fleet being concentrated ... resulting in economic concentration and market power ... Perhaps most important, ITQs can lead to increases in social class distinctions and severe problems with equity and social justice.
>
> J. Acheson, S. Apollonio, and J. Wilson, Individual transferable quotas and conservation.[3]

## 5.1 OVERFISHING: ECONOMIC PROPERTY RIGHTS AND COASE VERSUS RENT-SEEKING AND PRESCRIPTION

The argument in this chapter is that although US fishery regulation eventually bolstered stocks, the regulatory process was complex and slow, driven by costly rent-seeking. Economic theory had long described solutions to open-access fisheries. Templates existed for application of tradable use rights and potentially for user determination of annual harvest caps. Nevertheless, traditional prescriptive controls even under regional councils were maintained for twenty years before use rights as individual tradable quotas were adopted. Those use rights were influenced by rent-seeking objectives that limited access and alienability. These are examples of restricting entry and raising rivals' costs.

The problem of fisheries has always been overfishing due to open access. The Coasean solution would have been to assign property rights to fish or the right to fish and to allow fishers to determine

---

[2] Macinko, S. (1993). Public or private?: United States commercial fisheries management and the public trust doctrine, reciprocal challenges. *Natural Resources Journal*, 33 (4): 919–955, 924.

[3] Acheson, J., Apollonio, S., and Wilson, J. (2015). Individual transferable quotas and conservation: A critical assessment. *Ecology and Society*, 20 (4).

the total allowable annual harvests. Once in place, the rights would be exchanged to reduce the number of fishers and catch as well as to facilitate adoption of cost-effective technology, vessel size, and crews. That approach was not chosen in the Magnuson-Stevens Fishery Conservation and Management Act of 1976. Rent-seeking as defined here in stock management and in the design and distribution of property rights molded policy.[4]

Open-access fisheries require constraints on entry and harvest. Otherwise, there will be too many boats and fishers chasing too few fish. A race to capture increasingly valuable aquatic species inevitably results in overcapitalization, excessive crews, and rapid, but declining catches and incomes. Vessel owners and communities are placed at risk, as are biological fish stocks. The question then becomes the nature and effectiveness of the constraints.

One option is state-imposed regulations on who can fish as well as where, when, how, and amounts that can be caught. This is the centralized regulatory approach. As is evident, these controls require significant information by regulators on desired harvest levels, timing, vessel composition, and catches. It also requires investment in regulatory controls to ensure compliance. These restrictions do not assign ownership to any resulting aggregate fishery gains from forbearance. The race to capture them remains. It creates a setting for fishers to compete with one another within the regulations and as well as to outwit the regulators. Individual fisher incentives are to continue to over capitalize with more powerful vessels and greater storage capacity. More crew members may be required. This competitive imperative within centrally regulated fisheries leads to rising costs, falling harvest and incomes, and imperiled fish stocks. The regulatory response is to impose increasingly short fishing seasons and more onerous limits on who might fish and on their fishing inputs and yields.

---

[4] At risk species, ecosystems, and juvenile fish can be protected under a rights-based system. See Wallace, S., Turris, B., Driscoll, J., Bodtker, K., Mose, B., and Munro, G. (2015). Canada's Pacific groundfish trawl habitat agreement: A global first in an ecosystem approach to bottom trawl impacts. *Marine Policy*, 60 (10 : 240–248.

A second option is collective management within a group of fishers for selected fisheries. This approach follows from that outlined by Ostrom and summarized for natural resources in general by Cox et al.[5] There are attractions for group self-management, especially among some academics because it avoids assigning private property rights and a resort to markets that they criticize for equity and philosophical reasons.[6] It also can minimize the need for more direct government regulation.

Indeed, there are examples where small-group administration is successful.[7] At the same time, the conditions for such collective action to be effective, as described by Ostrom and Cox et al., often are overlooked by proponents, and yet, they are critical. These include bounded resources where borders can be monitored for entry and compliance. Migratory ocean fisheries do not meet this requirement. Another condition is that the group is relatively small and homogeneous in resource objectives and cost with little or no entry. Once again, valuable migratory species exploited by numerous fishers from various places, using different vessels, equipment, techniques, and crews, and potentially producing for different markets, violate this requirement. Commercial and recreational fishers also likely will have very different resource exploitation objectives along with production costs. Finally, group hierarchies may be quite different – more static in smaller, more remote communities, and more dynamic in larger ports. Entry, shifts in product mix, and changes in production

---

[5] Ostrom, E. (1990). *Governing the Commons*. Cambridge University Press. Cox, M., Arnold, G., and Tomas, S. V. (2010). A review of design principles for community-based natural resource management. *Ecology and Society*, 15 (4). December.

[6] Young, O. et al. (2018). Moving beyond panaceas in fisheries governance. *Proceedings of the National Academy of Sciences of the United States of America* 115 (37): 9065–9073. A notable critic of property rights is Daniel W. Bromley. For example, see (2011). Sufficient reason: Volitional pragmatism and the meaning of economic institutions. *Economica*, 78 (310): 391–392; and (2011). Abdicating responsibility: The deceits of fisheries policy, *Fisheries Magazine*. 9 January.

[7] See, for instance, local groundwater management within water conservation districts in Nebraska. Edwards, What lies beneath?; and Acheson, J. M. (1988). *The Lobster Gangs of Maine*. University Press of New England.

methods are encouraged by rising fish prices, shifting capital costs, new consumer demands, and technological change. These dynamics challenge local arrangements and make them less effective in larger scale fishery management.

The most economically attractive and effective option is the assignment and enforcement of economic property rights in the fishery and their exchange to reduce the number of fishers and vessels. Because property rights assign the benefits and costs of fishery management to rights holders, these fishers have incentives to adjust operations to maximize long-term economic yields and to protect fish stocks. Individual incentives for depletion inherent in an open-access fishery are removed. Moreover, rights holders and markets respond to new information about production methods, capital, and consumer demand. Because even migratory ocean fisheries tend to be found in specific waters based on temperature, feed, and spawning areas, regional decentralized negotiated solutions to overfishing are feasible.

These potential socially valuable outcomes follow from Coase, who implicitly outlined the motivation of parties to negotiate control of overfishing externalities; Demsetz, who described the natural adjustment of economic property rights with rising fish values; and H. Scott Gordon, Anthony Scott, and Francis T. Christy, who defined the role of property rights as the remedy to fishery open access.[8]

In light of serious overfishing and various options to choose from, the Magnuson-Stevens Fishery Conservation and Management Act was enacted in 1976, *twenty-two* years after Gordon and *sixteen* years after Coase, enough time and reason for employing property rights in fisheries. Along with its reauthorizations in 1996 and 2006, the law was and remains the principal US law to address overfishing, protect stocks, and improve economic and biological conditions.[9]

---

[8] Coase, The problem of social cost; Demsetz, Toward a theory of property rights; Gordon, The economic theory of a common-property resource; Scott, The fishery; Christy, Fisherman quotas.

[9] Public Law 94–265, 1976, 90 Stat. 331; Public Law 104–297 1996, 110 Stat. 3559; Public Law No: 109–479 121 Stat. 3575, 2007.

Unfortunately, the value-creating institutional reforms suggested in the economics literature described in Chapter 2 to address the problems of open-access fisheries generally were not the first responses, nor when adopted, did the property rights include key attributes critical for efficiency: security, durability, and transferability. Fishery rights were not implemented until 1990 and 1992 in three US fisheries, with further fishery rights placed on hold in 1996 for five *more* years. Ultimately, the rights allowed under the law were deemed not to be a legal property right, but a temporary use right, revocable without compensation. Further, the allocation and trade of the rights was targeted to specific parties, and exchange was constrained. These conditions lowered both the value of the property institution and its ability to address the losses of the commons.[10] Finally, the total cap on harvests was *not* set by fishers with insights from fishery biologists and a weighing of costs and benefits, as would have been recommended by Coase or Ostrom, but by regulators to meet biological objectives, usually to control harvests to be consistent with maximum sustainable yield. Fishers are influential in this process, but it is not the negotiated cap with property rights as suggested by Coase.

Magnuson-Stevens created regional management councils as a forum for more localized problem-solving, such as setting annual caps on harvest by species. Figure 5.1 shows the regional management councils organized around local fisheries and fishing interests.

Unfortunately, the law authorized a wide range of interests beyond those actually fishing to be members of the councils. This in itself is not problematic if the parties had tradable instruments so

---

[10] Reiser, A. (1997). Property rights and ecosystem management in U.S. Fisheries: Contracting for the commons symposium – The ecosystem approach: New departures for land and water: Fisheries management. *Ecological Law Quarterly*, 24: 813–833; Strong, J., and Criddle, K. R. (2013). *Fishing for Pollock in a Sea of Change: A Historical Analysis of the Bering Sea Pollock Fishery.* Alaska Sea Grant, University of Alaska Fairbanks; Grainger, C. A., and Costello, C. J. (2014). Capitalizing property rights insecurity in natural resource assets. *Journal of Environmental Economics and Management*, 67 (2): 224–240.

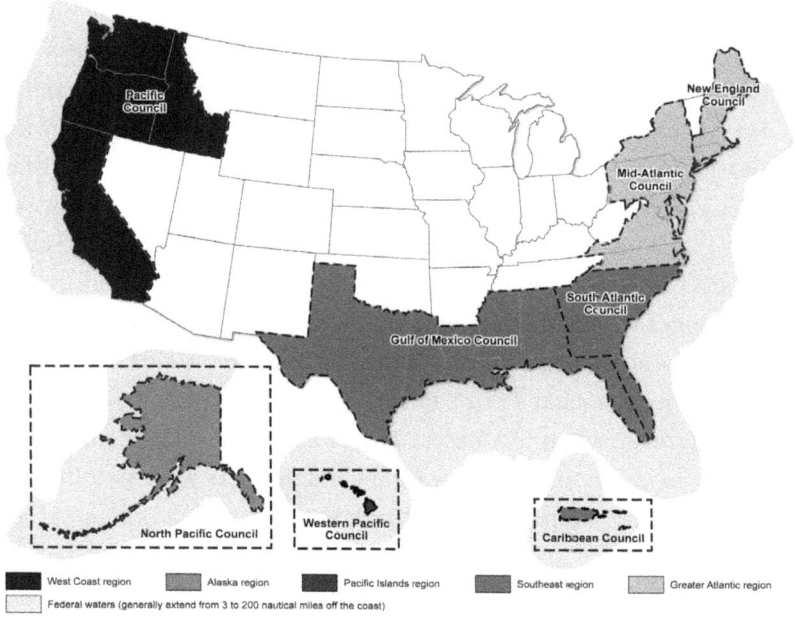

FIGURE 5.1  Regional fishery management councils.
*Source:* Congressional Research Service (2023), US Regional Fishery Management Councils. R47645 (https://congress.gov/crs-product/R47645, Figure 1).

that exchange could take place among the varied parties. Accordingly, they did not have property rights to the relevant stocks, nor did they share pecuniary objectives in fishery management. As a result, while an improvement over the Clean Air Act and its uniform national standards, for example, the makeup of the regional councils and the absence of fully exchangeable fishery rights within them has complicated fishery management. Agreement on conservation approaches often has been difficult and members have not been residual claimants to transaction cost efficiencies. When these incentives are absent, more economically beneficial institutions are not put into place.

Indeed, as we see with other environmental policies, economic costs and returns have played a secondary role in the regulations, relative to biological concerns and political sensitivity to the impact of property rights and markets on traditional fishery practices and communities. Under the Magnuson-Stevens Act, management measures "shall, where practicable, consider efficiency in the utilization of fishery resources; except that *no* such measure shall have economic allocation as its sole purpose." Although the adoption of limited fishery rights was a clear improvement over past input regulation, as described in this chapter, they were distributed to politically favored constituencies and their exchange limited to avoid major new changes in the makeup of fleets, vessel sizes, employment, and community structures.[11] With limits on property rights trade, any inefficiencies associated with initial assignment could be locked in with long-term economic losses. The challenge in this chapter is to explain why economic property rights and markets were so inhibited despite potential aggregate economic fishery gains.

## 5.2 THE ECONOMIC PROBLEM: ECONOMIC AND BIOLOGICAL OVERFISHING

There has long been a need for property rights in fisheries. The planet's oceans have been the last commons. For centuries, fishers used well-known and relatively primitive technologies in chasing and harvesting rich fish stocks. Although open access, historic fishing pressure by coastal state fleets was too limited and sporadic to do much damage. Once on shore, there also were high transportation and storage costs for marine harvests, driving down demand. Even through the nineteenth century with new vessel designs, fuels, and capture technologies, most fish stocks remained at limited risk from overharvest.

Very highly valued whales, of course, were an exception. Initially, stocks were huge, but as mammals that had to surface

---

[11] See, for example, Wilson, J. A., Acheson, J. M., Metcalf, M., and Kleban, P. (1994). Chaos, complexity and community management of fisheries. *Marine Policy*, 18 (4): 291–305; Acheson, J. M. (2015). Private land and common oceans: Analysis of the development of property regimes. *Current Anthropology*, 56 (1); and Young, Moving beyond panaceas. See also discussion of political responses to the distributional effects of assigning property rights in Macinko, Public or private?

to breathe, whales could be spotted, chased, and harpooned. As described by Herman Melville in his 1851 classic *Moby Dick*, the global race for whales led them to be harvested in the tens of thousands by whaling-vessel crews annually over the nineteenth and early twentieth centuries. By the 1930s, competitive slaughter had depleted once seemingly inexhaustible whale populations, driving up costs and lowering catches and returns. Petroleum had displaced whale oil in most markets, but the damage had been done. Only by the early twenty-first century did most whale stocks rebound thanks to various international restrictions on harvest and reduced demand.[12]

Migrating ocean fish populations faced similar pressures when the end of World War II set off a renewed and more intense race to fish. Military investment in vessels and related gear led to spinoffs resulting in lower-cost harvests, longer distant-water fishing fleets, greater harvest depths, and advanced fish storage and processing. Radar and sonar made locating fish concentrations more effective and improved weather prediction lowered risk to fleets and crews. New opportunities emerged for previously less-exploited demersal and pelagic species. Moreover, the ravages of the war led to a concerted search for new sources of protein for human populations. Finally, as economies recovered and per capita incomes rose, demand jumped for newly desirable fish for direct consumption or as feedstocks for poultry and livestock as well as fertilizer for agriculture.

Poul Holm, for example, outlines the rapid rebound of effort after World War II in the rich fisheries of the North Atlantic that were soon faced with overfishing, as shown in Figure 5.2.[13] The ocean was open for entry by fleets from all over Europe. Within two years after the end of the war, fish landings in Northern Europe equaled or exceeded peak levels of 1939, and that was just the beginning.

---

[12] Costello, C., Gaines, S., and Gerber, L. (2012). A market approach to saving the whales. *Nature*, 481: 139–140.

[13] Holm, P. (2012). World War II and the "Great Acceleration" of North Atlantic fisheries. *Environment and Society Portal*.

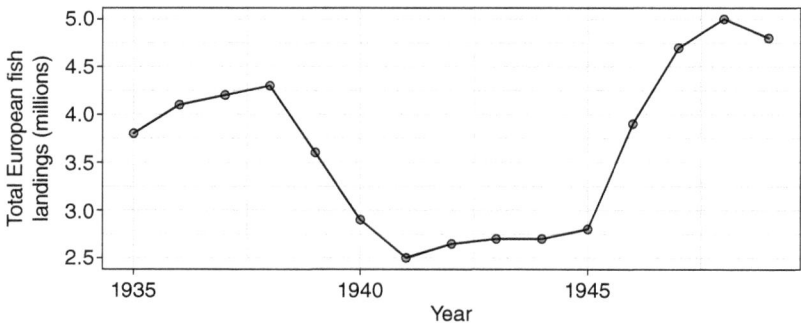

FIGURE 5.2 North Atlantic fish landings, 1935–1949.
Source: Calculated from data in Holm, World War II and the "Great Acceleration," 69.

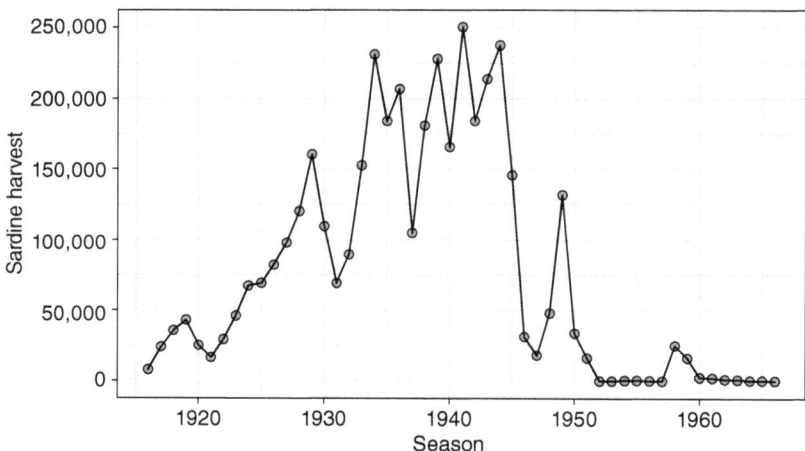

FIGURE 5.3 Monterey sardine harvest, 1916–1967.
Source: Calculated from data in Ueber and MacCall, The rise and fall of the California sardine empire, 3. Harvest is in tons of Sardines.

Another example illustrates even more dramatically the potential for biological stock and economic rent depletion with open access, namely the collapse of the Monterey Bay, California sardine fishery. Figure 5.3 details the buildup and collapse of landings from 1916–1967. Once one of the country's most valuable fisheries with canneries lining the Monterey waterfront and immortalized in John Steinbeck's 1954 book *Cannery Row*. The fishery provided canned sardines for direct human consumption, meal for poultry feed and fertilizer, and fish oil.[14] At the peak, there were hundreds of vessels and 101 fish-reduction plants in California in addition to canneries.[15] It was a significant source of income and value, offsetting the effects of the national economic depression. Vessels fished and unloaded at Monterey and other ports or to factory or reduction ships beyond the territorial three-mile state regulatory limit.[16] Landings rose dramatically through 1946 and then plummeted.

With virtual open access, harvests went beyond what could be sustained by the sardine biomass, and dwindling stocks were vulnerable to changes in water temperatures related to exogenous shocks like El Niño. A moratorium on landings was not implemented until 1967. In the rush to harvest dwindling supplies, fishers raced to beat one another, and one fisher who participated in the last season in 1968 stated: "In the last year we caught them all in one night."[17] An eighty-year-old fishery, once a source of wealth for many, collapsed with one remaining fisher in 1968.[18] The dangers of open access in fisheries were clear. What did we know from economic theory about how to confront them?

## 5.3 HOW TO ADDRESS OPEN ACCESS IN FISHERIES: THE THEORY

While fishery stocks were being depleted in the post WWII period, economic theories of needed institutional remedies appeared. Gordon and Scott described open-access incentives and their property rights

---

[14] Ueber, E. and MacCall, A. (2013). The rise and fall of the California sardine empire. NOAA 92104.
[15] Ueber and MacCall, The rise and fall of the California sardine empire.
[16] Radovich, J. (1982). The collapse of the California sardine fishery: What have we learned? *California Cooperative Oceanic Fisheries Investigations Report*, XXIII, 57.
[17] Quoted by Ueber and MacCall, The rise and fall of the California sardine empire, 35.
[18] Radovich, The collapse of the California sardine fishery, 61; and Ueber and MacCall, The rise and fall of the California sardine empire, 42.

solutions.[19] Christy took their arguments further by calling for a Total Annual Allowable Catch (TAC) in a fishery and assigning catch shares within it as a property right.[20] Distribution generally would be based on historical harvests (grandfathering).[21] The amount of fish available for each shareholder would depend upon the TAC, which for Christy would be based upon biological stock assessments. He did not examine a more critical weighing of economic costs and benefits in setting up the TAC. Even so, catch shares of the TAC, assigned to fishers as individual quotas, would be freely transferable as individual transferable quotas (ITQs). More generally beyond fisheries, as we have seen, Coase and Demsetz detailed the value of economic property rights and suggested how well-defined property rights and markets were superior to prescriptive regulation in reducing waste and advancing economic welfare.[22]

With the fishery closed to all but owners whose shares were valuable only so long as the relevant stocks were protected, the incidence of and incentives for overharvest would be reduced. There would be no need to race for fish. With tradable shares, the number of fishers, vessels, and related equipment and crews could be reduced as needed in any overcapitalized fishery. The most talented and skilled fishers would remain, and the sellers would gain the value of their relinquished shares. As with other economic assets, entry by new fishers could occur through the purchase of shares, financed via mortgages or other tradable assets.[23] With shares secure, they could serve as collateral and be passed along to heirs. With a property

---

[19] Gordon, The economic theory of a common-property resource; Scott, The fishery.
[20] Christy, Fisherman quotas.
[21] Anderson, T. L., Arnason, R., and Libecap, G. D. (2011). Efficiency advantages of grandfathering in rights-based fisheries management. *Annual Review of Resource Economics*, 3: 159–179.
[22] Coase, The problem of social cost. Demsetz, Toward a theory of property rights. Demsetz, The core disagreement.
[23] Sean Hartnett describes how families and friends helped tenants finance land sales in similar settings on the nineteenth-century US frontier. See: The land market on the Wisconsin frontier: An examination of land ownership processes in Turtle and LaPrairie townships, 1839–1890. *Agricultural History*, 65: 38–77.

rights system, there were potentially self-enforceable controls among owners on entry and compliance.

Because share values depended upon product value and production costs, owners had an incentive to search for new techniques, lower-cost vessels, more effective gear, and new markets with higher-valued fish products. As argued by Christy:

> It is the essential element of this suggestion for fisherman quotas that fishermen have as much freedom as possible to take their quotas in whatever way they wish. Given this freedom, valuable technological innovations would be encouraged rather than impeded or prohibited ... In essence, the fisherman quota scheme provides the fishermen with property rights in the resource itself. They have a share of the resource which they are free to use in any way they see fit subject to minor conservation restraints. The right might even be sufficient to use as collateral for obtaining loans.[24]

Scott et al. outline critical attributes of these quota shares or ITQs as a property right: (a) Security – the catch share would be protected by the state and its legal system; (b) Exclusivity – share owners would determine production and investment with incentives to cooperate with other share owners; (c) Transferability – the share would be freely marketable; (d) Divisibility – the share could be divided and exchanged as with any property; and (e) Durability – the share would be a long-term asset.[25] With property rights, investment, production, and exchange could take place to maximize economic returns and not be affected by the race to fish.

---

[24] Christy, Fisherman quotas, 3, 4.
[25] Scott, A. (1999). Moving through the narrows: From open access to ITQs and self-government. In Shotton, R. (ed.), Use of property rights in fisheries management, *FAO Fisheries Technical Paper* 404/1. 105–118. Arnason, R. (2020). Property rights as a means of economic organization. In Shotton, R. (ed.), Use of property rights in fisheries management. *FAO Fisheries Technical Paper* 401/1; Runolfsson, B. Th. (2024). Measuring quality of property rights: Development of user rights quality in the Icelandic fisheries. *Marine Policy*, 160, February, 105962. For complete overview of ITQs, see Arnason, Individual transferable quotas in fisheries.

Indeed, there has been documented success of ITQs or catch shares as property rights in improving stocks and fishery incomes.[26] Iceland and New Zealand, two nations that depended critically on their fisheries and conservation of the stock, adopted ITQs in 1975 and 1986, respectively.[27] However, political opposition among constituencies in the US resulted in ITQs being placed on hold, with a more abbreviated rollout that included controls on distribution, design, and exchange. As previously noted, the US placed a five-year moratorium in 1996 on additional ITQs beyond the few already implemented. As indicated later, rent-seeking to promote distributional objectives and philosophical concerns were powerful obstacles to adopting economic property rights and in affecting the kinds of rights that could be applied.

## 5.4 REACTION TO OPEN ACCESS: REGULATORY CONTROLS AND LIMITED PROPERTY RIGHTS

### Failure of Limited Entry Regulation

Initial responses to the race to fish were not aligned with established economic theory for addressing open access in fisheries. Hannesson describes a general pattern of moving from uncontrolled entry to prescriptive government regulation and finally to the adoption of property rights with their efficiency advantages.[28] The first global institutional change to the race to fish was to extend the control of coastal states over adjacent seas. These were initially by decree in the US and Canada in 1976, and then through international agreements among other countries under the Law of the Sea of 1982.

---

[26] Arnason, R. (2007). Fisheries self-management under ITQs. *Marine Resource Economics*, 22 (4): 335–451; (2008). Iceland's ITQ system creates new wealth. *Electronic Journal of Sustainable Development*, 1 (2): s. 35–41; (2012). Property rights in fisheries: How much can individual transferable quotas accomplish? *Review of Environmental Economics and Policy*, 6: 217–236. Costello, C., Gaines, S. D., and Lynham, J. (2008). Can catch shares prevent fisheries collapse? *Science*, 321 (5896): 1678–1681.

[27] Individual catch shares were granted in the Icelandic herring fishery in 1975 and made fully transferable in 1979.

[28] Hannesson, R. (2006). *Privatization of the Oceans*. MIT Press.

As boundaries were extended from 3 to 12, and finally to 200 miles, countries could control entry by foreign fleets. These extended areas became country exclusive economic zones (EEZs).[29] Within them, however, domestic fleets, generally subsidized, soon replaced foreign ones, and intensive fishing pressure resumed.

The 1976 Magnuson-Stevens Fishery Conservation and Management Act was designed to protect and develop US fisheries by excluding foreign fleets from entrance within a 200-mile zone and regulating US fishing.[30] Eight regional fishery management councils were established and charged with drafting and implementing fishery management plans. Except in a few cases, these plans did not include property rights and relied upon various limited entry and output controls.

Even so, as noted earlier the regional management councils provided a forum for assembling various interests in drafting regional fishery plans. By providing a framework for such negotiations, this provision in the law is more Coasean and the councils might have provided the structure for defining more complete property rights, had that been the objective.[31] As we have seen in Chapter 4, there is nothing similar in the administration of the Clean Air Act that delegated policies to regional bodies for setting air quality standards and potentially addressing local regulatory costs and benefits. Unfortunately, the Magnuson-Stevens Act is an outlier among US environmental legislation that typically designates uniform restrictions at the behest of national lobby groups, politicians, and agencies. Regional fisheries seemingly were better organized along local characteristics to affect policies within the political process.[32]

Overall, the US and Canada implemented various controls within their EEZs to restrain internal entry and harvests. Limited

---

[29] See Hannesson, *Privatization of the Oceans*, 23–24, for initial EEZs and p. 173 on inefficiencies and constituencies in the subsequent rights adopted.
[30] PUB. L. NO. 94-265, 90 Stat. 331 (1976) (codified at 16 U.S.C. §§ 1801–1884).
[31] Dan Holland, Senior Scientist, Northwest Fisheries Science Center, NOAA pointed this to me.
[32] See Libecap, State regulation of open-access, common-pool resources.

licensing schemes were designed to define the number of vessels allowed in each regulated fishery. Fishers were still motivated by the race to fish and responded by making their licensed vessels more powerful with more storage space. No fisher or regulator was a residual claimant to any enhanced economic value in the fishery from compliance. Overall, harvests did not decline. Regulators responded by adding other limits on net sizes and trawls. These, too, were adapted around. Total harvest quotas were set, and seasons were put into place to enforce them. Even so, a marathon of fishers leaped into the fishery as seasons opened, sprinting to the best locations. Information about stock locations became critical.[33] Annual quotas were quickly met, and although seasons were shortened by regulators, vessel owners invested in more capital and crews to lead the race.

Each new restriction to suppress fishing led fishers to further private efforts to outmaneuver competitors and regulators. Regulators were driven by the biological objectives of stock preservation, politicians by the demands of political constituencies, and fishers by the economic imperatives of meeting vessel mortgage payments, paying crews, and earning incomes for their families.

Most observers concluded that the 1977 extension of the 200-mile limit by the Magnuson-Stevens Act failed to halt overfishing. New England groundfish stocks collapsed as fleet capacity quickly exceeded the total harvest quotas, which were withdrawn with Congressional pressure on the regional Fishery Management Council. Catch per unit of effort plummeted. In 1996, the New England Council had twenty-six stocks under management, of which twelve were overfished. A conservation biology approach in limited licensing management did not address the fundament economic problem of fishers and their incentives.[34]

---

[33] Johnson, R. N. and Libecap, G. D. (1982). Contracting problems and regulation: The case of the fishery. *American Economic Review*, 72 (5): 1005–1022.

[34] Observers like Rieser, Property rights and ecosystem management; and Crestin, D. S. (2000). Federal regulation of New England fisheries: A different point of view.

The experience of the Pacific Northwest halibut fishery of the US and Canada illustrates the fishery dilemma with regulation in the absence of a property rights regime. The relevant data patterns provided in Grafton et al. for the British Columbia fishery also applies to the US because the stocks were migratory and the fleets were similar, only partitioned by national ocean boundaries between the US and Canada.[35] Limited licensing regulations implemented in Canada in 1980 allowed for a maximum of 435 vessels. There also were additional gear restrictions and minimum fish size rules. Although designed to enhance the stock, increases in biomass from regulation made entry and expansion within the limited licensing scheme even more attractive.[36]

After 1980, a fishing derby arose as fishers competed by adding vessels, crews, and times spent fishing. The number of vessels rose quickly from 333 in 1980 to the limit of 435 by 1988, when total harvest peaked at 12,859,562 pounds, up 128 percent from 1980. Older vessels were withdrawn, and were replaced by new, more efficient ones within the maximum. Pressure on the stock grew and stock assessments indicated sharp declines. Regulators were forced to take their only option of reducing the allowable season. By 1990 the season had shrunk to *six* days from sixty-five. In the US portion of the fishery, the season was *four* days in 1984.[37] For the remainder of the year, vessels, captains, and crews shifted to other fisheries, perhaps overexploiting them, or waiting idle, accruing capital and potential labor costs.

The aggregate costs were obvious. Moreover, the value of the harvest declined. With a very short fishing season, the catch had to be

---

Symposium Proceedings: History, Status, and Future of the New England Offshore Fishery. *Northeastern Naturalist*, 7 (4): 337–350.

[35] Grafton, R. Q., Squires, D., and Fox, K. J. (2000). Private property and economic efficiency: A study of a common-pool resource. *Journal of Law and Economics*, 43(2): 679–714.

[36] Homans, F., and Wilen, J. (2005). Markets and rent dissipation in regulated open access fisheries. *Journal of Environmental Economics and Management*, 49 (2): 381–404.

[37] Karpoff, J. M. (1987, 191). Suboptimal controls in common resource management: The case of the fishery. *Journal of Political Economy*, 95 (1): 179–194.

stored frozen for the rest of the year, denying consumers higher valued fresh fish.[38] Finally, beyond excessive fishing costs and reduced market value, there were lost gear, equipment conflicts, higher discard rates for non-target species, and increased hazards in fishing.

Catch shares as ITQs were introduced in the British Columbia portion of the fishery in 1991 and in the Alaskan portion in 1995, just prior to the Magnuson-Stevens moratorium. Through quota exchanges, the number of vessels gradually declined; the stock rebounded; and the season was extended, reaching 245 days in British Columbia by 1993. Absent the need to race, fishing took place according to market demand; fresh fish were supplied, not frozen; and the number of processors was reduced.[39]

Across fisheries, there was general dissatisfaction with limited licensing, which could not reverse the decline in stocks or return fisheries to profitability.[40] Fixed-gear fishers blamed mobile-gear fishers; small vessel operators blamed large; inshore blamed offshore; recreational fishers and environmental groups blamed commercial fishing. Congressional buyouts of licenses did not attract experienced fishers, termed "high liners." As noted earlier, various property rights options, such as shares of the total allowable harvest, were considered. Individual or group quotas for each fishery and area to vessel owners, owners and crews, processors, and community groups were contemplated. Controversies continued over initial allocation, capitalization and concentration, conservation, safety, efficiency, employment and community, and wealth generation.[41] Ultimately, limited entry regulation largely was replaced by property rights regimes, although not as ideal economic property rights.

---

[38] See also Huppert, D. W. (2005). An overview of fishing rights. *Reviews in Fish Biology and Fisheries*, 15: 205–206.
[39] Grafton et al., Private property and economic efficiency.
[40] Sustainable Fisheries Act, PUB. L. NO. 104-297, 110 Stat. 3559 (1996) (amending 16 U.S.C. §§ 1801–1884).
[41] Many of these issues are described by Buck, E. H., and Waldeck, D. A. (2005). The Magnuson-Stevens Fishery Conservation and Management Act: Reauthorization Issues. *Congressional Research Service*, February 7.

## Property Rights Constituency Positions and Political Limitations

Table 5.1 summarizes the positions of key parties during Congressional Hearings on the 1996 reauthorization of the Magnuson-Stevens Act. The assessments of commercial, sports/recreational fishers, environmental NGOs, politicians, and regulatory officials are included. Although the economic and biological benefits of property rights regimes are acknowledged by some, the distributional impacts for others were more serious, and they looked to politically imposed rights assignments and associated rents. Others philosophically objected to the privatization of any government resource. These stands affected the way in which property rights were defined in the different regions and fisheries covered by the law.

Table 5.1 includes testimony from four management regions: North Pacific because it had a large commercial sector but also some active small fishing communities in Alaska; Mid-Atlantic because it was the first region to adopt a property rights program and had both active commercial fisheries and a large recreational industry; New England because it included many diversified fisheries that represent both small and large commercial fisheries; Gulf of Mexico because it had considerable commercial, sport, and recreational fishing industries and was one of the last management regions to adopt catch shares.[42]

Mobilization of political pressure and related rent-seeking via assigned and restricted property rights made it difficult to implement ITQs in a more direct way. Given conflicting constituency positions outlined in the hearings, politicians considered a sunset on all catch shares after seven years, followed by reallocation. It was not implemented. Instead, any new fishery property rights

---

[42] Total Testimonies, New England–Boston: 12, Rockport: 25; North Pacific–Anchorage: 48, Seattle 40; Gulf of Mexico–New Orleans: 20; Mid Atlantic–Charleston: 12, Morehead City: 18.

Table 5.1 Constituency sentiments regarding catch shares property rights

North Pacific[a]

| classification | Sentiments | Main points |
|---|---|---|
| Large commercial fishers | Overall, in favor | Controls entry; reduces competitive loss of gear and bycatch |
| Small commercial fishers | Overall, strongly opposed | Offered fishing shares based on historical catch too small for economic viability; vessel/share combinations lead to loss of vessel management by captains; shares migrate to banks and foreigners; harms fishing communities, natives |
| Recreational fishers | Overall, against | Small shares lead sport-fisher migration to near shore, harming stocks; charter-boat owners with offshore sport fishing restricted |
| Politicians/government agency officials | No clear sentiment, but considerable concern about constituent impact | Uncertainty about impact on fisheries and small operators; acknowledge conservation potential |
| Environmental NGO members | Overall, against | Shares alone will not conserve stock; need regulation; shares force out small fishers and threaten communities |

New England[b]

| classification | Sentiments | Main points |
|---|---|---|
| Large commercial fishers | Overall, in favor | Shares provide incentives to invest in fisheries |
| Small commercial fishers | Overall, strongly against: | The diverse lobster industry has small operations; shares are too small to be viable; consolidation by large companies |
| Politician/government agency | Overall, for: | Conservation benefits to be captured by shareholders; management costs need recovery |
| Environmental NGO members | Overall, against: | Opposed privatizing a public resource; rewards those who do not fish conservatively with most shares; encourages discarding. Profits attracts more fishing |

Mid-Atlantic[c]

| classification | Sentiments | Main points |
|---|---|---|
| Large commercial fishers | Overall, for | Promotes conservation and fishery stability; opportunity for more shares if stocks grow; rewards those who sell |

| | | |
|---|---|---|
| Small commercial fishers | Overall, against | Low seafood prices and limited shares to small fishers harms them more than large fishers; catch shares encourage consolidation; creates monopolies; calls for moratorium |
| Recreational fishers | Mixed | Advantages commercial fishers over recreational and sports; may promote conservation |
| Politician/government agency | Overall, for | Current surfclam and ocean quahog ITQ proves ITQs work and should be expanded; ITQs with other conservation efforts lead to healthier fisheries |

Gulf of Mexico[d]

| classification | Sentiments | Main points |
|---|---|---|
| Large commercial fishers | Ambivalent | Guidelines not robust; lack clarity; need moratorium |
| Small commercial fishers | Overall, strongly against | Shrimp fisheries manage themselves; ITQs neither designed correctly nor equitably; create unfair competition; non-fishers acquire permits |
| Recreational fishers | Overall, against | Hurts small fishers and charter-boat operators; smallest driven out; guidelines unclear. Uncertainty |
| Politician/government agency | Overall, for | Need to cover management costs; funds can be used to address equity concerns |

Notes:

[a] S. 39, hearing on the reauthorization of the Magnuson-Stevens Fishery Conservation and Management Act: Hearing before the Subcommittee on Oceans and Fisheries of the Committee on Commerce, Science, and Transportation, United States Senate, One Hundred Fourth Congress, first session, March 25, 1995, Anchorage, Alaska. U.S. Department of Commerce. (n.d.). https://shorturl.at/8SlV2.

[b] S. 39, hearing on the reauthorization of the Magnuson-Stevens Fishery Conservation and Management Act: Hearing before the Subcommittee on Oceans and Fisheries of the Committee on Commerce, Science, and Transportation, United States Senate, One Hundred Fourth Congress, first session, March 4, 1995, Boston, Massachusetts. U.S. Department of Commerce. (n.d.). https://shorturl.at/ppTuz.

[c] United States. (1995). S. 39, Reauthorization of the Magnuson-Stevens Fishery, Conservation, and Management Act: hearing before the Subcommittee on Oceans and Fisheries of the Committee on Commerce, Science, and Transportation, United States Senate, One Hundred Fourth Congress, first session, July 15, 1995, Charleston, South Carolina. U.S. G.P.O.: For sale by the U.S. G.P.O., Supt. of Docs., Congressional Sales Office. https://catalog.hathitrust.org/Record/009798229.

[d] S. 39, hearing on the reauthorization of the Magnuson-Stevens Fishery Conservation and Management Act: hearing before the Subcommittee on Oceans and Fisheries of the Committee on Commerce, Science, and Transportation, United States Senate, One Hundred Fourth Congress, first session, May 13, 1995, New Orleans, Louisiana. Note. (1995). S. 39, Hearing on the Reauthorization of the Magnuson-Stevens Fishery Conservation and Management Act: Hearings before the Subcommittee on Oceans and Fisheries of the Committee on Commerce, Science, and Transportation, United States Senate, One Hundred Fourth Congress, First Session, May 13, 1995, New Orleans, Louisiana. 1, 1-198. https://heinonline.org/HOL/P?h=hein.cbhear/hrmfcv0001&i=1.

arrangements in the US were paused, *ten* years after New Zealand's ITQ system and approximately *seventeen* years after Iceland's fully tradable ITQs were put into place. A Gulf of Mexico red snapper ITQ under consideration was halted, but the Mid-Atlantic surf clam and ocean quahog individual fishing quota (IFQ) and South Atlantic wreckfish IFQs continued.

Ultimately, the 1996 reauthorization of Magnuson-Stevens, called the Sustainable Fisheries Act, or SFA, defined ITQs or catch shares as narrow usufruct permits for harvest that could be revokable or limited at any time without compensation, and may or may not be renewed: "shall not create, or be construed to create, any right, title or interest in or to any fish before the fish is harvested."[43] Under the law, individual fishing quotas or catch shares had exclusivity, at least for the term, but transferability was limited, and durability was at risk.[44] Conditions were placed on ITQ trading to reduce vessel consolidation in some fisheries and to retain a small vessel, community-based fishery.[45] In 2006, the Magnuson-Stevens Fishery Act was reauthorized with more emphasis on limited catch shares or ITQs.[46]

---

[43] 16 U.S.C. § 1853a(b), (16 USC as amended 110 Stat 3576-77.

[44] Courts have held that fishing licenses and permits do not function as property protected by the Fifth Amendment Takings Clause. *American Pelagic Fishing Company v. U.S.*, 379 F.3d 1363 | *Casetext Search + Citator.* (n.d.). https://casetext.com/case/american-pelagic-fishing-company-v-us. *Conti v. U.S.*, 291 F.3d 1334 | *Casetext Search + Citator.* (n.d.). https://casetext.com/case/conti-v-us-2. One court described the permits not as a property right but as "one measurement of current investment and recent participation in, and dependence upon, the fishery" *PACIFIC DAWN, LLC v. PRIT* | *No. C13-1419 TEH.* | *20131209610* | *Leagle.com.* (n.d.). Leagle. https://www.leagle.com/decision/infdco20131209610.

[45] Singh, R., Weninger, Q., and Doyle, M. (2006). Fisheries management with stock growth uncertainty and costly capital adjustment. *Journal of Environmental Economics and Management*, 52 (2): 582–599. Weninger, Q., and Singh, R. (2010). Fleet restructuring, rent generation, and the design of individual fishing quota programs: Empirical evidence from the Pacific Coast groundfish fishery. *Marine Resource Economics*, 24: 329–359, January 2010.

[46] Magnuson-Stevens Reauthorization of 2006 PUB. L. NO. 109-479, 120 Stat. 3575 (2007). See Craig, R. K., and Danely, C. (2017). Federal fisheries management. *Journal of Land Use and Environmental Law*, 32 (2): 381–422, at 396–397.

In light of regulatory restrictions and uncertainty, most US catch share programs have very thin markets with high participation costs, undermining their efficiency.[47] There are economic consequences. Grainger and Costello compare dividend price ratios (lease price/sales price) for catch shares in the US, Canada, and New Zealand, and find that the ratios were significantly higher in the US with riskier sales and more reliance upon leases, than in New Zealand where clearer property rights existed.[48] Given these constraints, what are the property rights in US fisheries?

## 5.5 PROPERTY RIGHTS IN US FISHERIES

Table 5.2 lists catch shares for sixteen fisheries, year adopted, types, and constraints on allocation, holdings, and exchange. The property rights institutions vary. They include community development quotas (CDQs), individual fisher quotas (IFQs), Cooperative Quotas, IPQs or individual processor quotas, and ITQs. They differ according to the assignment of fishing rights, timing, and restrictions on transferability.

CDQs are granted to Western Alaska natives with little fishing experience to contract with actual fishers via annual leases. Cooperative fishing quotas are delegated to members with share transfers only within the group. IFQs and ITQs allow for broader short-and long-term exchanges (leases and sales) but they typically are subject to a variety of limitations that differ across fisheries. These include total share accumulation limits, mandated onboard captain exchanges, requirements for inclusive crew and captain trades, total vessel capacity maximums (smaller not larger vessels), and vessel quota permit limits.[49] Processor fishing quotas may be transferred, but often only among processors.

---

[47] Holland, D. S. et al. (2015). US catch share markets: A review of data availability and impediments to transparent markets. *Marine Policy*, 57 (C): 108–109.
[48] Grainger and Costello, Capitalizing property rights insecurity.
[49] Holland et al., 103–110, table 5.2.

Table 5.2 US fishery property rights

| Region | Fishery | Catch share type* | Year implemented | Separable, divisible, and transferrable? | Restrictions |
|---|---|---|---|---|---|
| North Pacific | Western Alaska CDQ | CDQ | 1992 | N/A | Ownership traded within the community; 10% of total quota; individual shares can be expanded or revoked |
| | Halibut and Sablefish | ITQ | 1995 | Yes, but limited | Individually allocated; revoked with inactivity;[a] quota shares within regulatory area and transferable only among same vessel class[b] |
| | Bering Sea American Fisheries Act Pollock | Group co-op | 1999 | Yes, but limited | Named vessels harvest within co-ops; shares not transferable across sectors |
| | Bering Sea/Aleutian King & Tanner Crab | ITQ/IPQ, can be co-op | 2005 | Yes, but limited | Shares to owners/crew and processors; species-/area-specific shares; regional delivery; revokable if inactive; transfer requires prior experience[c] |
| | Bering Sea/Aleutian Non-pollock Groundfish Trawl | Individual within co-op | 2008 | Restricted | Quota shares and transfers only to co-op members[d] |
| | Freezer Longline Conservation Cooperative | Co-op | 2010 | Restricted | Shares/transfers only to co-op members |
| | Central Gulf of Alaska Rockfish | Individual within co-op | 2012 | Restricted | Co-op shares/transfers only to vessels within quota |
| Pacific | Pacific Coast Fixed Gear Sablefish | ITQ | 2001 | Yes, but limited | Owner on board only; with individual quota |
| | Pacific Coast Groundfish Trawl | Individual ITQ/co-op | 2011 | Yes, but limited | Separate area shares; no transferability across inshore/at-sea sectors; aggregation limits |

| Region | Fishery | Type | Year | Transferable | Notes |
|---|---|---|---|---|---|
| New England | General Category Atlantic Scallops | ITQ | 2010 | Yes, but limited | Scallop-vessel owners only; none across sectors; aggregation limits[e] |
| New England | Northeast Multispecies Groundfish | Individual within co-op | 2010 | Restricted | Shares/transfers within co-op |
| Mid-Atlantic | Surfclam and Ocean Quahog | ITQ | 1990 | Yes | Transfers from ITQ holders[f,g] |
| Mid-Atlantic | Mid-Atlantic Golden Tilefish | ITQ | 2009 | Yes | Aggregation limit |
| South Atlantic | South Atlantic Wreckfish | ITQ | 1992 | Yes | Aggregation limit |
| Gulf of Mexico | Red Snapper | ITQ | 2007 | Yes | Transfer within total individual quota[h,i] |
| Gulf of Mexico | Grouper and Tilefish | ITQ | 2010 | Yes | Transfers within total individual quota[j,k] |

Notes:

[a] 50 CFR § 679.40 – Sablefish and halibut QS. (n.d.). LII / Legal Information Institute. www.law.cornell.edu/cfr/text/50/679.40.

[b] 7 Fed. Reg. 57130, 57136 (Dec. 3, 1992).

[c] Fisheries of the Exclusive Economic Zone off Alaska; Bering Sea and Aleutian Islands Crab Rationalization Program; C Shares. (2022, July 15). Federal Register. https://shorturl.at/QEzCP.

[d] 50 CFR 679.41 – Transfer of Quota Shares and IFQ. (n.d.). www.ecfr.gov/current/title-50/part-679/section-679.41.

[e] Fishery Management Guide – Part 11 : Limited Access Fisheries. (n.d.). https://masglp.olemiss.edu/fisherymanagement/part11/.

[f] Fisheries, N. (2023, May 30). Atlantic Surfclam and Ocean Quahog | NOAA Fisheries. NOAA. www.fisheries.noaa.gov/permit/atlantic-surfclam-and-ocean-quahog.

[g] Atlantic Surfclam and Ocean Quahog. (2024, January 26). Mid-Atlantic Fishery Management Council. www.mafmc.org/scoq.

[h] 50 C.F.R. § 622.21(a).

[i] 50 CFR § 622.21 – Individual Fishing Quota (IFQ) Program for Gulf Red Snapper. (n.d.). LII / Legal Information Institute. www.law.cornell.edu/cfr/text/50/622.21.

[j] 50 C.F.R. § 622.21(a).

[k] 50 CFR § 622.21 – Individual Fishing Quota (IFQ) Program for Gulf Red Snapper. (n.d.). LII / Legal Information Institute. www.law.cornell.edu/cfr/text/50/622.21.

Source: https://media.fisheries.noaa.gov/2023-09/FEUS-2020-final2-web-0.pdf; Holland et al., US catch share markets, figure 1.

## 5.6 CONCLUSION: POLITICAL RENT-SEEKING AND CONSTRAINTS ON ECONOMIC PROPERTY RIGHTS AND MARKETS

What have we learned from this dive into fishery property rights and the absence of a straightforward Coasean framework for addressing overfishing? Much of the material will be familiar to those who study the details of fisheries. Still, the emphasis here is on a broader issue: How political rent-seeking constrains the adoption of property rights and market exchange with its important welfare implications. The objectives of rent-seeking are not judged. Rather, the efficiency implications for US fisheries and economic returns fishers are the concern. Although fisheries constitute less than 0.8 percent of US GDP, they are critical for many populations. Because of their small presence, the aggregate costs of inefficient institutions within them are apt to be ignored among the overall population. Broad welfare effects depend upon the institutional arrangements to address open access. The record in the US has been mixed and certainly not what one might have anticipated given the extensive literature on the benefits of fishery property rights.

Gordon, Scott, Christy, Coase, and Demsetz described clear ways of addressing the economic costs of open-access resources through property rights assignment and their exchange in markets. The way in which things played out, however, provides cautionary insights for institutional formation when rent-seeking is prominent. Fisheries historically were part of an unconstrained commons. Effective remedies to the race to fish required property rights. They were not the first responses, however, nor were they implemented smoothly and completely when adopted. Instead, they were added only after centralized regulations failed. In most cases multiple contingencies lobbied politicians for the design, assignment, trading restrictions, and other attributes of the rights granted. These were designed to limit entry and raise rivals' costs. The outcome was not well-defined property rights with their efficiency and welfare potentials.

Discussions about the usefulness of Coasean approaches to address externalities are part of an extensive literature, mostly concerned with the interpretation and impact of transaction costs.[50] Key in the debate is the definition of transaction costs and what factors are included in the concept. Traditional transaction costs of definition, enforcement, and exchange affect the supply of property rights. The institutions observed, however, are also determined by the demand for them. The opportunity to mold property rights assignment via lobbying in the political process is critical, especially when property rights previously had not existed, as was the case in fisheries. This setting generated a perfect opportunity for various groups to advance their interests in the process via rent-seeking. Had property rights remained exchangeable, then the long-term economic impacts would have been mitigated. One-time wealth transfers would have occurred, but the rights would have migrated via trade to the most efficient fishers and regions. Given the constraints placed on assignment and transferability, however, this corrective process has been inhibited. In light of the small aggregate costs imposed, property rights reform may be a long time coming. Fisheries may remain relatively inefficient, and communities linked to them are poorer than otherwise might have been the case.[51]

Because property rights are political institutions, politicians negotiated how to insert them into previously unowned, but regulated fisheries. Political positions depended on short-term constituent support.[52] If the fishery had had a cohesive constituency,

---

[50] Medema, The Coase theorem at sixty; Dahlman, D. (1979). The problem of externality. *Journal of Law and Economics*, 22 (1); Barzel, *Economic Analysis of Property Rights*; and Barzel and Allen, *Economic Analysis of Property Rights*; Allen, What are transaction costs?

[51] Sutherland, S. A., and Edwards, E. C. (2022). The impact of property rights to fish on remote communities in Alaska. *Land Economics*, 98 (2): 239–253.

[52] Because the state was involved and the regulated constituency was fragmented with varying aims, political priorities were key. Public Choice, as detailed by Stigler, Peltzman, Olson, Buchanan and Tullock, points to the imperative of short-term horizons held by politicians seeking to reward key constituencies and the incentives of

the message to politicians would have been more straightforward, and the political response closer to a clear property right. This may explain the early and less constrained property rights in the Atlantic Wreckfish fishery in 1992. It was a new fishery with similar vessels and fisher objectives than existed elsewhere in other US fisheries where a greater mix of vessel sizes, aims (commercial, sports, recreational), and ports predominated. Where the latter characteristics were present, constituencies were more complicated, and political responses to property rights were more complex, with competing lobbying for favorable rights design and distributions. Political sponsors could provide compromised property rights that benefited key constituencies with policy-based rents, while any aggregate losses would be broadly spread across the US economy in the short term.

Parts of the regulatory bureaucracy may have had less incentive to experiment with new property rights regimes.[53] Among agency fishery biologists, long-term economic returns provided by property rights likely were of less concern than stock conditions. Greater agency budgets and mandates provided them with more regulatory latitude. Finally, NGO members, consultants, and academic researchers with no direct income links to the fishery, in some cases appear to have had interests more in line with traditional fishers, communities, and operations.

The experience of US fisheries illustrates how Coase and Williamson's efficiency-based property rights and organizational

---

tenured bureaucracies with discretion and little financial concerns at risk. Interest group organization and lobbying play crucial roles. Peltzman, Toward a more general theory of regulation; Olson, *The Logic of Collective Action*; Stigler, The economic theory of regulation; Buchanan and Tullock, *The Calculus of Consent*; Becker, A theory of competition among pressure groups; Laffont, J. J., and Tirole, The politics of government decision-making; and Johnson and Libecap, Information distortion and competitive remedies.

[53] Johnson, R. N. and Libecap, G. D. (1994). *The Federal Civil Service System and the Problem of Bureaucracy: The Economics and Politics of Institutional Change.* University of Chicago Press and NBER, 154–171.

innovations have held less attraction in policy.[54] The case of US fisheries, ideal for using economic property rights to confront open access and for keeping the industry abreast of changes in technologies, consumer demands, and biological conditions, did not meet that promise. Institutional reform in the policy arena provided too many options to channel rents politically.

[54] Coase, The nature of the firm; and Williamson, *Markets and Hierarchies* and *The Economic Institutions of Capitalism*.

# 6 Rent-Seeking in Protecting At-Risk Species
## *The Endangered Species Act (ESA)*

> It has become increasingly apparent that some sort of protective measures must be taken to prevent the further extinction of many of the world's animal species ...
>
> US Senate, Report on the Endangered Species Act 1973.[1]
>
> Nothing is more priceless and more worthy of preservation than the rich array of animal life with which our country has been blessed.
>
> President Richard Nixon, quoted in J. H. Adler, Tarnished gold.[2]
>
> A longstanding concern .... has been the relatively low number of listed species that have successfully recovered to the point where they no longer need protection.
>
> E. K. Eberhard, D. S. Wilcove, A. P. Dobson, Too few, too late.[3]
>
> The environmental camp ... has argued that the existing law must be strengthened ... The other camp has argued that the existing law is unduly onerous for those whose activities it regulates and must be made less so.
>
> Senate Environment and Public Works Committee concerning S.1180, the Endangered Species Act of 1997, September 23, 1997.

---

[1] Senate Report on the Endangered Species Act, 1973, 2. 93 Congress, Report No. 93-307: *Endangered Species Act of 1973, Report of the Senate Committee on Commerce on S. 1983 to Provide for the Conservation, Protection, and Propagation of Species or Subspecies of Fish and Wildlife That Are Threatened with Extinction or Likely within the Foreseeable Future to Become Threatened with Extinction and for Other Purposes.*

[2] Quoted in Adler, J. H. (2024). Tarnished gold: The Endangered Species Act at 50. *Florida International University Law Review*, 18 (2). Symposium: Environment Forum: From Science to Public Policy, 1.

[3] Eberhard, E. K., Wilcove, D. S., and Dobson, A. P. (2022). Too few, too late: U.S. Endangered Species Act undermined by inaction and inadequate funding. *PLOS ONE* 17 (10) (October 12).

> [T]he highest level of assurance that a property owner will not face an ESA issue is to maintain the property in a condition such that protected species cannot occupy the property ... This is ... the "scorched earth" technique.
>
> National Association of Home Builders, Developer's Guide to Endangered Species Regulation (1996).[4]

## 6.1  INTRODUCTION: DECENTRALIZED COASE OR CENTRALIZED PRESCRIPTION AND RENT-SEEKING IN SPECIES PRESERVATION

### Arguments in the Chapter

Saving some species from extinction can be a public good. Doing so is costly, however, diverting resources from other valuable activities. If attention is directed to those species that have reasonable recovery potential and the costs are not too great, then the resources might be well spent. If they are devoted to those that have little chance for recovery, possibly at high economic cost, then the exercise may be less beneficial. Proponents might argue that all species deserve a chance, but because real resources are involved, people are affected. They must support funding and costly resource-use restrictions over very long periods to list, protect, and enhance at-risk species. There are opportunity costs. The hard choices about which species to protect and how much to pay for them involve tradeoffs that impact human populations. The process of endangered species protection then ought to be a reasoned one that weighs costs and benefits, even in light of very difficult information and data problems. There is no avoiding the challenge. Unfortunately, as detailed in this chapter, protecting endangered species has not been a reasoned process. It is contentious and combative. The record of success is extremely sparce. Rent-seeking appears to undermine chances for long-term recovery for prospective species.

[4] Quoted in Lueck, D., and Michael, J. A. (2003). Preemptive habitat destruction under the Endangered Species Act. *Journal of Law and Economics*, 46 (1): 27–60, 27.

Rent-seeking under the Endangered Species Act (ESA) delivers psychic, nonpecuniary returns to proponents, reelection benefits to some politicians, and budgets and mandates for affected regulatory agencies. Public goods also can be delivered, although the values and net returns vary dramatically across the population. For some the benefits are large, such as the ability to observe the return of the wolf population in Yellowstone, whereas for others the costs are large, such as for those whose jobs were lost with restrictions on logging in forests affected by the presence of spotted owls.

Overall, rent-seeking has raised the costs of protecting at-risk species; has made the process of listing or delisting species under the law controversial; has inflicted disproportionate costs and benefits across the citizenry; and has instilled incentives among private landowners, who hold most species, to preemptively destroy habitat. As documented, few species have recovered, although listings for protection under the law continue to grow. Because the law's range is small compared to the Clean Air Act, for example, its overall costs are limited, although not for directly affected parties. Despite intense backing from supporters, the ESA is reviled by others. This is an unfortunate outcome for efforts to save the nation's at-risk species.

Importantly, preexisting legislation relied upon Coasean decentralized methods to secure critical habitat, and that might have been a more promising pathway. Rent-seeking objectives among political agents instead led to controversial prescriptive controls under the law.

## A Decentralized Approach Not Taken

The quotations above capture the promise, failing, and controversy surrounding the Endangered Species Act of 1973 (Pub. L. No. 93-205, 87 Stat. 884). There is an enormous academic and policy literature associated with the law, perhaps more than any other environmental legislation.[5] Given its narrow thrust relative to the Clean Air

---

[5] Mann, C. C., and Plummer, M. L. (1995). *Noah's Choice: The Future of Endangered Species*. Knopf.

or Clean Water Acts, for example, and its apparent limited accomplishments, this attention may be surprising. It reflects, however, the provocative nature of the legislation with its prescriptive regulatory approach to saving species at risk of extinction.[5] It also mirrors concern among some citizens about the loss of endangered species. Finally, it reflects the ability of advocates to secure government directed policy rents and related strongly held preservation objectives by claiming species protection as public goods. These policy outcomes are largely paid for by narrowly regulated parties, populations in communities where natural resource use has been curtailed, and general taxpayers.

This chapter examines the legislative histories, economics, politics, and outcomes of the ESA to show why mandates were adopted and have been maintained, despite their probable limited benefits for target species or broad citizen welfare. There clearly can be broad public gains from directing some resources to avoiding, where feasible, species extinctions. Although Coase did not address problem of extinction, it certainly fit within the range of externalities outlined by him.[7] If private parties acted in ways that threatened the existence of some species, not weighing those costs would result in excessive land-use practices and habitat destruction. In such cases, those with economic property rights would bear opportunity costs in failing to capitalize on the rising value of critical plants, birds, and animals, as well as disregarding the impact of their practices that were of concern to others, who would be willing to pay for change.

There *was* potential for Coasean exchange, certainly within the narrow spatial setting and limited number of parties involved that characterizes most endangered species and habitats in the US. If offered compensation, landowners would have incentives to modify property uses or be willing sellers. They might adjust cropping

---

[6] Pigou, A. C. (1920). *The Economics of Welfare*. Macmillan.
[7] Endangered species often are open-access resources. See Cheung, The structure of a contract.

and grazing patterns, avoid the harvest of some old growth timber stands, change irrigation water diversions, move mining operations, or modify location and density of housing construction. At the same time, members of environmental NGOs, other parties, and government agencies responding to organized citizen demands would be willing payers, remunerating landowners for desirable adjustments in resource use.

Landowners would receive the incremental net benefits for areas sold, leased, or set aside from damaging production. Conservationists would receive the incremental net benefits from the designation of areas as critical habitat or calls for other changes in behavior. The exchange would take place so long as preservationists perceived value equal or exceeding what landowners demanded as compensation and so long as landowners perceived monetary gains from incremental adjustments in land uses. Negotiated outcomes could be flexible with ongoing trade adjustments to new costs and benefit information. With additional evidence on species status (locating other previously unknown stocks or indications of greater peril), buyers could secure more land or devise additional ways of paying for additional conservation efforts. Similarly, with new land value information (shifts in prices or costs, new products, or services) sellers could offer alternative production adjustments or locations and reenter negotiations to free up land. In theory at least, the process could be elastic, long lasting, and not contentious.

With a decentralized Coasean approach, conservation would be a joint effort, not a regulatory tax on one party. Both buyers and sellers would have a stake in the exchange and its outcome. They would be partners in preservation. Landowners or government land leaseholders would be collaborators, not coerced parties, or labeled as perpetrators in species decline. Endangered species could be assets and worthy of active protection efforts. Such partnership could promote durable government or NGO funding as required for long-term recovery.

Monetized species protection could elicit the cooperation of those who knew most about the land and who must adjust behavior as part of proposed conservation. They would have less incentive to preemptively harvest or to engage in land uses that potentially harmed the species. That type of behavior would mean foregoing value if there were the option of Coasean exchange. Moreover, and perhaps even more fundamental, the requirement for trade would force both parties to confront opportunity costs. Bargaining would balance marginal willingness to accept (value of foregone land uses or costs of other behavioral adjustments) and marginal willingness to pay (value of protecting species). Marginal costs and benefits could be matched.

Importantly for social and political cohesion as well as long-term collaboration, the two parties would *not* have to place the same values on species or ecosystems. Conservation would not be primarily a question of ethics or morality. Such concepts are very difficult to exchange or to adjust in resource use decisions, and they can be very socially and politically contentious. Even with recognition of value judgements in avoiding extinction, such judgements will vary. While some parties might be willing to bear serious costs, others might not. Indeed, as Elinor Ostrom's work has pointed out, common views on natural resource use and protection are more likely to be found within small, homogeneous groups and where costs and benefits are assessed similarly and borne proportionately.[8] Under more realistic larger national settings, the parties would not have to have "shared visions" about addressing threats to at-risk species. There would be no need to castigate those who seemingly were less concerned, or evaded protections due perhaps to bearing higher costs. Coasean exchange would be most useful when there were differences in views. Those differences would fuel trade.

The tricky problem of benefit measurement also would be addressed in the exchange. Environmental NGOs and relevant government agencies would weigh their acquisition and management costs with their anticipated gains. More easily measured costs could set

---

[8] Ostrom, *Governing the Commons*.

a benchmark as to the anticipated value from preservation. Benefits would have to at least equal costs, or benefits/costs would have to be equal to or greater than one for any level of land exchange to attract the interest of conservation purchasers and be welfare improving.[9]

A vital outcome of voluntary bargaining would be a more equitable distribution of the costs and benefits of endangered species preservation. Landowners, who would have to change their resource use and bear the costs of doing so, would not bear a disproportionate cost share relative to any private benefits they gained from preservation. Advocates with high preservation values would achieve desired land-use outcomes while paying for them. When policy costs and benefits are not distributed proportionately, some parties will get more than they pay for, and others less than they receive in policy benefits. The latter will be aggrieved and resist or undermine conservation. For species at risk, such behavior could be very damaging.

There *was precedent* for expanded Coasean approaches to species conservation. By the late 1960s, biologists were aware that most terrestrial endangered species were at risk because of habitat loss. There was growing use of easements and land trusts for voluntary, compensated conservation.[10] More importantly, the precursors of the 1973 ESA, the Endangered Species Preservation Act of 1966 (Pub. L. No. 89-669, 80 Stat 926) and the Endangered Species Conservation Act of 1969 (Pub. L. No. 91-135, 83 Stat. 275) focused on the acquisition of land as habitat by expanding the National Wildlife Refuge System. The 1969 law also authorized the Secretary of the Interior to develop a list of species or subspecies of animals that were threatened with extinction. This list could have been a basis for identifying key habitats for purchase. Indeed, the 1973 statute freed up funding for

---

[9] See benefit measurement approach taken in Ovando, D., Libecap, G. D., Millage, K. D. and Thomas, L. (2021). Coasean approaches to address overfishing: Bigeye tuna conservation in the Western and Central Pacific Ocean. *Marine Resource Economics* 36 (1): 91–109.

[10] Farmer, J. R., Knapp, D., Meretsky, V. J., Chancellor, C. and Fischer, B. C. (2011). Motivations influencing the adoption of conservation easements. *Conservation Biology* 25 (4): 827–834.

habitat acquisition from the Land and Water Conservation Fund, the Migratory Bird Conservation Act, the Fish and Wildlife Act of 1956, and the Fish and Wildlife Coordination Act. and other sources.[11]

Moreover, private property rights to land existed for much of the country, where most endangered species were found in total or in part, and most federal and state lands were privately distributed and used under long-term grazing leases, logging concessions, oil and gas and mining permits. This setting meant that exchange could take place, avoiding the transaction costs, economic losses, and other rent-seeking outcomes encountered with fisheries in the assignment of property rights, examined in Chapter 5. A Coasean approach with economic property rights to species preservation was both feasible and had precedence. It was not taken. Political rent-seeking dominated. Prescriptive controls, not decentralized bargaining resulted.

Figure 6.1 shows a map of critical habitat for listed species under the Endangered Species Act. As revealed, critical habitat tends to be local and generally small, enabling bargaining and purchase. Some species cover wider ranges, such as the spotted owl in the Pacific Northwest so that larger terrain might have been required. An advantage of actually having to pay for habitat is that it would have required those who sought protection to carefully define the areas required. Under the political/administrative process such precision may not be required. Proponents do not bear the costs of habitat set asides.

An essential problem with rent-seeking is that imposed policies can be inefficient, ineffective, inequitable, and, as a result, potentially defeating. ESA advocates use the regulatory authority of government to achieve their desired normative or biologically based policy goals without a balancing of associated economic costs and benefits and or confronting the incentive and economic effects of the observed imbalance. The setting likely has led to too much protection of unsalvageable species, to too many uncompensated private

---

[11] Bean, M. J. and Rowland, M. J. (1997). *The Evolution of National Wildlife Law*, 3rd ed. Praeger. 194–198, Senate Hearings, 2–3. House Hearings, 9.

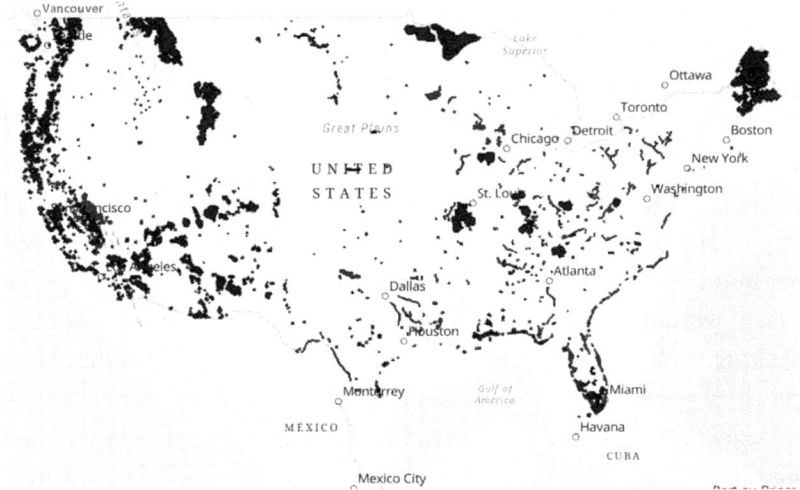

FIGURE 6.1 Critical habitat.
*Source:* US FWS. https://shorturl.at/dLxsa.

costs on landowners and other affected parties, and to a political reaction that might ultimately unravel conservation goals.[12]

With rent-seeking it is difficult to answer the question of how far restrictions on private resource use should go. For advocates, they should go far enough to bring the target species back from the edge of extinction. Who could place a value on avoiding extinction? The costs involved would be those necessary to achieve the goal. Saving endangered species was a moral imperative, a social obligation. Indeed, in 1978, in *Tennessee Valley Authority* v. *Hill*, the U.S. Supreme Court held that the ESA explicitly placed species conservation above other social goals when goals were in conflict. The court held that: "The plain intent of Congress in enacting this stature was to halt and reverse the trend toward species extinction, *whatever the cost*" (437 US 153, 184. 1978, italics added).

---

[12] See the political response to the declaration of large-scale marine protected areas (MPAs) in Australia, displacing existing fishing and other economic activities. Libecap, G. D. (2024). Advancing ocean ecosystem conservation via property rights, rather than Marine Protected Areas (MPAs). *Maritime Studies*, 23 (March): Article 15.

## Environmental Concerns and Adoption of Prescriptive Controls under the Endangered Species Act

At the time the Endangered Species Act was enacted, there was growing consciousness among some segments of the population about the plight of at-risk species along with discussion about what to do about them. Per capita incomes had risen from $3,037 in 1960 to $5,234 in 1970, so that broader environmental demands could be addressed via higher levels of economic well-being and consumption/investment potentials.[13] Moreover, the US population had become more urban, 74 percent by 1970, fueling an attraction for rural, natural landscapes and species.[14] Awareness also was driven by rising education levels. In 1960, 41 percent of the population aged twenty-five years and over had a high school education, but by 1970, that share had risen to 55 percent.[15] Finally, the government share of GDP had risen from 9.6 percent in 1960 to 12.6 percent in 1970, raising experience and expectations about government's role in the economy.[16]

Indeed, there was alarm among some that the spread of human populations and economic activities were leading to the loss of seemingly treasured species and ecosystems.[17] As stated in the Senate Report on the ESA of 1973, 2: "The two major causes of extinction are hunting and destruction of natural habitat." There also was a sense for some that these imperiled resources might hold previously unrealized economic values in new drugs, pharmaceuticals, and food sources. The House Report on the ESA of 1973, 5, stated: "From the most narrow possible point of view, it is in the best interests of

---

[13] World Bank. www.macrotrends.net/global-metrics/countries/USA/united-states/gdp-per-capita.
[14] Historical Statistics of the United States, Millennial Edition Online, chapter Aa. https://hsus.cambridge.org/HSUSWeb/HSUSEntryServlet.
[15] US Census 1970.
[16] Government receipts and expenditures/GDP, US Census 1970.
[17] Wyman, K. M. (2008). Rethinking the ESA to reflect human dominion over nature. *New York University Environmental Law Journal*, 17: 490, See also Taylor, M. S., and Weder, R. (2024). The economics of extinction and possible mass extinctions. *Journal of Economic Perspectives*, 38 (3): 237–259.

mankind to minimize the losses of genetic variations. The reason is simple: they are potential resources."

A focus on the environment and endangered species was attractive politically as politicians and government agency officials sought new ways to address popular demands. Membership had grown in environmental organizations that supported collective action, such as the Sierra Club, World Wildlife Federation, Environmental Defense Fund, Natural Resources Defense Council, and the Nature Conservancy. Environmental NGOs could mobilize their relatively higher income, highly educated, and urban members of the citizenry to advance legislation and policy.[18] Further, as discussed in Chapter 2, there also was a conviction among some economists and politicians that market failure was a growing problem, particularly with control of externalities, highlighting an ostensible need for government remedy.

As noted by Bean and Rowland, beginning in the 1970s there was a powerful view among members of influential constituent groups that the environment, many natural resources, and wildlife should be protected by government intervention.[19] As such, these resources were to be held by the government to focus on broad public goods provision and not as economic property that might reflect narrow private interests and profit motives. This viewpoint was distinctly not Coasean, and it provided little opportunity for decentralized negotiation over the costs and benefits of the ESA.

This philosophical assessment is demonstrated by the Public Trust Doctrine (PTD), introduced in Chapter 4, which held that certain natural and cultural resources were inherently public, not

---

[18] The rise of environmental NGOs and the overall environmental movement is discussed by Coglianese, Social movements, law, and society. For discussion of the issues involved in interpreting poll data, see Berinsky, Measuring public opinion with surveys. There seemingly is surprisingly little information on membership characteristics and financial support of environmental organizations in the peer-reviewed literature. For basic information see: www.sierraclub.org/california/about-us.

[19] Bean and Rowland, *The Evolution of National Wildlife Law*.

private, and ought to be preserved by state prescription.[20] Although a prominent legal doctrine, there is no predictive model for testing about which resources would be singled out or if or when politicians and other government agents would act in the public interest, however defined rather than in reaction to narrower political self-interests or to the demands of partisan advocacy groups. There seemingly is no analytical public choice literature that critically examines the Public Trust Doctrine for its welfare implications.[21]

The Endangered Species Act has been labeled the most powerful environmental law in the country, if not the world.[22] This judgement follows from its strict prohibition of human actions that could harm targeted species and their habitats enforced by civil and criminal penalties. The statute may have prevented some extinctions, but recovery of listed species is very limited. What is clear is that the law has become a lightning rod, surrounded by rancorous debate.[23]

Incremental costs of listing more species under the law are not a critical factor under the ESA. Indeed, cost considerations in listings *are prohibited*, although some were allowed later via a 1978 ESA amendment for critical habitat designation. Such neglect of

---

[20] Bean and Rowland, *The Evolution of National Wildlife Law*, 7.
[21] Libecap, G. D. (2007). *Owens Valley Revisited: A Reassessment of the West's First Great Water Transfer*. Stanford University Press. He examines *National Audubon v. Superior Court* 33 Cal 3rd 419, 1983, where the court held that the state's obligation to manage water under the Public Trust Doctrine superseded prior appropriative water rights held by the city of Los Angeles in transferring water from the Mono Basin to the city. In its ruling, the court made the water a commons and potentially weakened private appropriative water rights, water transactions, and water values.
[22] Scott, J. Michael, Goble, Dale D., and Davis, Frank W. (2005). *The Endangered Species Act at Thirty, Vol. 1: Vol. 1: Renewing the Conservation Promise*. Washington, DC: Island Press. Owen, D. (2012). Critical habitat and the challenge of regulating small arms. *Florida Law Review* 64: 141. See also discussion and references in Adler, Tarnished gold, 2–3.
[23] See discussion in Wood, J. (2024). America's wildlife habitat conservation act, explained. Property and Environment Research Center, Bozeman, Montana. www.perc.org/2024/02/29/americas-wildlife-habitat-conservation-act-explained/; and Downey, H., Priest, J., Regan, S., Watkins, T., Wood, J., and Yablonski, M. (2023). *A Field Guide for Wildlife Recovery: The Endangered Species Act's Elusive Search to Recover Species – And What to Do about It*. Property and Environment Research Center.

costs can lead to too much protection, too few achievements, and too high social impacts of conservation – even if some species are saved from extinction. Absent compensation, parties facing regulatory constraints, but capturing only small portions of any global benefits, are made worse off, making the law inequitable. Overall, economic impacts have not been integral in endangered species policy design, which has been driven more by biology and the moral imperative asserted by proponents of avoiding extinction regardless of cost.

Although administration of the Endangered Species Act is not to consider economic costs in listings, but costs can become politically significant, as occurred when Congress overrode delays in the construction of the Tellico Dam in Tennessee. Construction had been halted by the U.S. Supreme Court in *Tennessee Valley Authority* v. *Hill* (437 US. 153, 172-73, 1978) in response to litigation spearheaded by a law student and an academic biologist about the dam's impact on the alleged endangered snail darter. In reaction to the dam controversy in 1978, Congress amended the ESA to require economic considerations in critical habitat declarations (not listings) along with other requirements.[24] Subsequently, the snail darter was found to have other populations, was moved from being categorized as endangered to threatened, and was finally delisted as recovered in 2022.[25]

Because the regulatory process does not require negotiated purchases, things can go too far. The possibility was illustrated by a 2018 U.S. Supreme Court case, *Weyerhaeuser Co.* v. *U.S. Fish*

---

[24] See: Congressional discussion of the Tellico Dam controversy in *A Legislative History of the Endangered Species Act of 1973*, as amended in 1976, 1977, 1978, 1979, and 1980: together with a section-by-section index / prepared by the Congressional Research Service of the Library of Congress for the Committee on Environment and Public Works, U.S. Senate.

[25] See Nark, J. (2025). This tiny fish's mistaken identity halted a dam's construction. Scientists say the snail darter, whose endangered species status delayed the building of a dam in Tennessee in the 1970s, is a genetic match of a different fish. *New York Times*, January 3, 2025. www.nytimes.com/2025/01/03/science/snail-darter-fish-tellico-dam.html.

*and Wildlife Service*.[26] The issue was the designation of extensive critical habitat for the endangered dusty gopher frog (listed in 2001) by the Fish and Wildlife Service (FWS). The FWS had designated 1,544 acres of private land as critical habitat even though the frog had not been found there. The court ruled that the action was excessive. Only land actually, and not prospectively, occupied by the species, could be considered critical habitat and subject to regulatory controls. The reversal in this case, however, still required that the affected landowner bear the costs of going to the Supreme Court to challenge the law.

Critical habitat designation can trigger a variety of land-use restrictions, permitting delays and environmental impact studies, raise the risk of embarking on construction projects that subsequently could be curtailed. One peer-reviewed study of the economic impact of critical habitat declaration for threatened or endangered species is by Auffhammer et al. They estimate the effect of critical habitat pronouncements on the market value of vacant land in central/northern California.[27]

The analysis was based on data from over 13,000 land transactions that occurred within or near critical habitat for the red legged frog and the Bay checkerspot butterfly. Since the frog was threatened by other invasive frog species and the butterfly by air pollution, critical habitat declaration may or may not have improved the species' recoveries. Even so, critical habitat designation for the frog decreased land values by an estimated 48 percent and by at least an estimated 78 percent for the butterfly. The largest impacts occurred within potential urban growth areas, possibly constraining housing development

---

[26] Congressional Research Service, *Home Is Where the Habitat Is: Supreme Court Addresses Critical Habitat under the Endangered Species Act*. December 19, 2018. The Supreme Court held that only actual habitat of an endangered species could be designated as critical habitat under the Endangered Species Act (ESA). See also Wood, J. and Watkins, T. Critical habitat's "private land problem": Lessons from the dusky gopher frog. *Environmental Law Reporter* 51 (7) (2021).

[27] Auffhammer, M., Duru, M., Rubin, E., and Sunding, D. L. (2020). The economic impact of critical-habitat designation: Evidence from vacant-land transactions. *Land Economics*, March 2020, 96 (2): 188–206.

in a region where housing supplies already were limited, prices high, and affordable housing access politically controversial.

In general, the economics literature that examines the economic impact of the ESA finds that single species listings and related critical habitat declarations in specific areas have negative impacts on vacant land and property values in affected markets. Studies include those by List et al. and Greenstone and Gayer.[28] Listing has led to documented declines in farmland values and employment in some affected counties.[29] A more recent analysis covering multiple species and sites and comparing parcels with identical histories of protection is by Frank et al.[30] They find considerable heterogeneity in ESA effects. Overall, they suggest that the aggregate land market impacts across affected areas could be small. The Endangered Species Act shifts market transactions from inside to outside the protected area and leads to a slight appreciation of residential and vacant land values beyond designated critical habitats.[31]

Uneven distributions of benefits and costs affect incentives to cooperate and political support for conservation.[32] An informative case occurred in Australia where there were extensive government designations of Marine Protected Areas (MPAs) in Australian coastal waters in the 1990s at the behest of conservationists concerned about at-risk aquatic species and ecosystem losses. Indeed, Australia's

---

[28] List, J. A., Margolis, M., and Osgood, D. E. (2006). Is the Endangered Species Act endangering species? *NBER Working Paper*, No. 12777. National Bureau of Economic Research; Greenstone, M., and Gayer, T. (2009). Quasi-experimental and experimental approaches to environmental economics. *Journal of Environmental Economics and Management*, 57 (1): 21–44.

[29] Melstrom, R. T. (2020). The effect of land use restrictions protecting endangered species on agricultural land values. *American Journal of Agricultural Economics*, 103 (1): 162; and Melstrom, R. T., Lee, K. and Byl, J. (2018). Do regulations to protect endangered species on private lands affect local employment? Evidence from the listing of the Lesser Prairie chicken, *Journal of Agricultural and Resource Economics*, 43: 346.

[30] Frank, E. G., Auffhammer, M., McLaughlin, D., Spiller, E., and Sunding, D. (2025). The cost of species protection: The Land Market Impacts of the Endangered Species Act. *NBER Working Paper*, No. 33352. National Bureau of Economic Research.

[31] Frank et al., The cost of species protection.

[32] Ostrom, *Governing the Commons*.

MPAs were the most widespread in the world. Most MPAs were designated as "no-take," meaning that fishing, oil and gas production, mining, and other human activities, beyond research or limited tourism, were prohibited generally without compensation. Intense political reaction to the MPAs and lobbying by fishing industry members and community representatives resulted in a subsequent political moratorium on Marine Protected Areas and their roll back in some places, even as advocates warned of potential biological harms.[33]

## 6.2 THE ENDANGERED SPECIES ACT (ESA)

The Endangered Species Act followed 1966 and 1969 legislation but employed a dramatic shift from previous decentralized land acquisition to directed nationwide constraints for safeguarding at-risk species. The ESA defined an endangered species as "any species which is in danger of extinction throughout all or a significant portion of its range." A threatened species was any "likely to become an endangered species within the foreseeable future throughout all or a significant portion of its range" (16 U.S.C. §1532). Three sections spell out the mandates under the Act:

1. Section 4 of the ESA required that listing decisions were to be based solely on the best available science *"without reference to possible economic or other impacts of such determination"* (italics added). Required critical habitat designation for listed species was added in a 1978 amendment that also allowed for economic factors to be weighed in habitat designation (although not in listings). Tension over weighing the two factors led to another amendment in 1982 that allowed for incidental (inadvertent) private takings of an endangered species with fewer or no penalties. The thrust of the law, however, remained focused on biological protection mandates and not on costs or their distribution.[34]

---

[33] Libecap, Advancing ocean ecosystem conservation via property rights, 15.
[34] Bean and Rowland, *The Evolution of National Wildlife Law*, 198–200. Congressional Research Service, The Endangered Species Act: Overview and implementation. The Endangered Species Act of 1973 (ESA; P.L. 93-205, 87 Stat. 884, 16 U.S.C. §§1531-1544).

2. Section 7 barred federal government agencies from actions that would "jeopardize the continued existence of any endangered species or threatened species" or destroy critical habitat for such species (16 USC§1536). This provision affected federal lands permit holders.
3. Section 9 prohibited any unauthorized "taking" of endangered species on private lands (16 USC §1538). Taking not only included killing, wounding, or capturing an endangered species, but also harming it by destroying or adversely modifying its habitat. Violators were subject to fines and other civil and criminal penalties. The prohibitive thrust of the law was clear. There is no reference to negotiation nor collaboration with parties critical for species recovery. "Blanket rules" to provide the same regulatory protections for threatened as for endangered species have been added, rescinded, and reimplemented over time, reflecting the adversarial nature of ESA mechanisms.

Key factors in determining whether a species is endangered or threatened include present or susceptible habitat loss, over exploitation, disease, predation, weak existing regulatory protection, and other human activities that could imperil the species. The Endangered Species Act's objective is to conserve species listed as endangered or threatened by using "all methods and procedures which are necessary to bring any endangered species or threatened species to the point at which the measures provided pursuant to this chapter are no longer necessary."[35]

The law prohibited activities of government agencies and private individuals that could threaten at-risk species. The Secretary of Interior was to compile lists of target species with information provided through petitions from private individuals, academic ecologists and conservation biologists, as well as by government agencies and members of environmental groups,

No senator and only four members of the House of Representatives voted against the bill. As noted by Doremus: "Legislators appear to have regarded it as an opportunity to deliver ringing

---

[35] Adler, Tarnished gold, 9.

rhetoric that would please the environmental movement without facing any immediate political costs."[36] At the time, saving species was generally popular, with no sense of the potential for recovery nor of the costs necessary to achieve it. Voters in urban areas could view the Endangered Species Act favorably. More rural federal land permittees and private property owners were not only dispersed, but few likely would have anticipated the broad sweep of the law or of its ramifications.

This political consensus, however, would not survive as over time the cost/benefit tradeoffs and their different distributions became clearer. Politicization developed between supporters of the law and those who feared unpaid constraints and uncertainty on their land uses and values. As a result, the ESA has not been formally reauthorized since 1988. Efforts to amend and reauthorize the law, such as the Young/Pombo Bill in 1995, H.R. 2275, have not made it out of committee for a Congressional vote.[37] Other than a minor Defense Department amendment in 2004, limiting critical habitat declaration on military bases, no other ESA legislation has been enacted. Mired in disagreement, funding has been constrained by congressional opponents.[38]

Ando examines the listing process that often takes considerable time.[39] She finds that the timing of listings is affected by interest group lobbying. Delay can be harmful if it allows preemptive, irreversible

---

[36] Doremus, H. (2010). The Endangered Species Act: Static law meets dynamic world, Washington University. *Journal of Law and Policy*, 32: 175, 177.

[37] Hearing before the Committee on Resources House of Representatives One Hundred Fourth Congress First Session on H.R. 2275 A Bill to Reauthorize and Amend the Endangered Species Act of 1973 20-707CC September 20, 1995 – Washington, DC Serial No. 104-37.

[38] Adler, Tarnished gold, 12. On persistent underfunding, see also Eberhard et al., Too few, too late.

[39] Ando, A. W. (1999). Waiting to be protected under the Endangered Species Act: The political economy of regulatory delay. *Journal of Law and Economics*, 42 (1): 29–60; (2001). Economies of scope in endangered-species protection: Evidence from interest-group behavior. *Journal of Environmental Economics and Management*, 41: 312–332; (2003). Do interest groups compete? An application to endangered species. *Public Choice*, 114: 137–159.

actions on land that would be protected once the listing is made. Conservationists have an incentive to lobby for more rapid action, while those potentially bearing the costs from agency restrictions have an incentive to slow listings that could otherwise lower property values or reduce local employment. Lobby pressure is largely directed to key members of Congress holding seats on reauthorization subcommittees and Fish and Wildlife Service (FWS) funding committees.[40]

In addition to lobbying, litigation can force the FWS to designate listings. Langpap analyzes litigation by environmental NGOs to compel listing, critical habitat designation, and funding for imperiled species.[41] Such organizations file hundreds of lawsuits, and he finds that litigation accelerates or expands listings, critical habitat designation and size, as well as recovery expenditures for targeted species. Funding is important because FWS spending correlates with greater chances of recovery.[42] With agency budgets constrained, outlays are focused on politically driven species rather than on those most apt to respond and be delisted under the law.[43] Listing without added agency expenditures can have adverse consequences for species recovery by signaling to land holders of forthcoming agency action. Ferraro et al. suggest that using scarce conservation funding in the contentious process of listing may be less effective than using the

---

[40] Ando, Waiting to be protected; Ando, Do interest groups compete?; Economies of scope in endangered-species protection.

[41] Langpap, C. (2022). Interest groups, litigation, and agency decisions: Evidence from the Endangered Species Act. *Journal of the Association of Environmental and Resource Economists*, 9 (1): 1–26. Langpap points out that lawsuits have grown dramatically over 1990–2016. See also Langpap, C., Kerkvliet, J., and Shogren, J. F. (2018). The economics of the U.S. Endangered Species Act: A review of recent developments. *Review of Environmental Economics and Policy* 12 (1): 69–91; and Langpap, C., and Shimshack, J. P. (2010). Private citizen suits and public enforcement: Substitutes or complements? *Journal of Environmental Economics and Management*, 59 (3): 235–249.

[42] Kerkvliet, J., and Langpap, Christian. (2007). Learning from endangered and threatened species recovery programs: A case study using U.S. Endangered Species Act Recovery scores. *Ecological Economics* 63: 499.

[43] Ferraro, P. J., McIntosh, C., and Ospina, M. (2007). The effectiveness of the U.S. Endangered Species Act: An econometric analysis using matching methods. *Journal of Environmental Economics and Management*, 54: 245, 246.

funding to promote recovery for more viable ones.[44] For litigants and lobbyists, however, listing is a primary objective because it places the species within the ESA's regulatory umbrella.

Positions of participants in Congressional Hearings on the Young/Pombo reauthorization and ESA reform bill, HR 2275, in 1995 illustrate the divide between critics and supporters of the law. Table 6.1 summarizes the positions and testimony of members of groups critical or supportive of the ESA. Their statements speak past one another and are not responsive to opponents' points. The narratives make clear that the Endangered Species Act was not enacted as a Coasean negotiated approach for species preservation.

Table 6.1 reveals no common ground. This is the result of policy rents, provided by politicians and agency officials to key constituencies, that are mandated and not tradable. It could be possible to negotiate over implementation approaches to reduce costs and garner some political support, but the habitat directives, based on legislation and agency actions, are not generally adjustable via bargaining between conservationists and landowners. Some negotiated arrangements have occurred within aspects of the ESA, but the principal ESA restrictions remain.[45]

A 1982 amendment in Section 10 of the law allowed for incidental takings permits for private landowners to cover small-scale activities that might cause minor, inadvertent taking of listed species in private land-use actions. The permits required an approved habitat conservation plan that may also include securing offsetting credits from a habitat bank. These provisions were designed to encourage private partnership in species protection. Other programs to boost cooperation included candidate conservation agreements and safe harbor agreements. Such programs are to provide regulatory assurances to landowners to conserve a species without the threat of more land-use controls if their actions expand the target's population and range.

---

[44] Ferraro et al., The effectiveness of the U.S. Endangered Species Act.
[45] For general discussion, see Costello and Kotchen, Policy instrument choice with Coasean provision.

Table 6.1 Positions by interest groups on the 1995 reform and reauthorization of the Endangered Species Act (ESA)

| Group | Science | Costs | Regulatory agency | Property rights | ESA successful? |
|---|---|---|---|---|---|
| ESA critics: Property Groups; Farm Bureau; American Forest and Paper Association; Society of American Foresters; Chamber of Commerce; Holmes Western Oil; Mining Representatives; Competitive Enterprise Institute; Farm Water Alliance; Weyerhaeuser, Inc; Pacific NW Lumber Mills; Timber Industry Representatives; United Paper workers International Union; Other Labor Groups; Benjamin Cone, Jr., Greensboro, North Carolina; National Wilderness Institute; and others | Focus on species that could be saved, not all at-risk species with little chance of recovery; critical habitat to be where species are found and might recover | Costs placed on property owners; species preservation has costs that should be borne by taxpayers and advocates | Create a National Biodiversity Reserve from federal lands, easements, purchased and leased lands | Property rights infringed. Takings. Law creates perverse incentives | No |

| ESA supporters: | Proposed creation of biological reserves | Cost of land purchases and compensation | An alternative biological reserve law | Did not directly address | Yes |
|---|---|---|---|---|---|
| Pacific Coast Federation of Fishermen's Associations; Sierra Club; Environmental Defense Fund; Ecological Society of America; National Research Council; Stuart Pimm, Department of Ecology and Evolutionary Biology, University of Tennessee; Michael Bean, Chair, Wildlife Program, EDF; and others | biological reserves through purchase will substitute politics for scientific/biological considerations for determining listings and critical habitat; species have intrinsic value; biodiversity should not be lost; critical habitat declaration to follow biological recommendation and species requirements | too great and would undermine administration of the law | would limit ability of regulatory agencies to carry out ESA mission | | |

*Source:* Drawn from testimony and position statements at Congressional Hearings: Hearing Before the Committee on Resources House of Representatives One Hundred Fourth Congress First Session on H.R. 2275 A Bill to Reauthorize and Amend the Endangered Species Act of 1973 20-707CC September 20, 1995. Washington, DC Serial No. 104-37.

These collaborative efforts, while laudable, however, do not change the underlying coercive nature of the ESA in Sections 4, 7, and 9, as previously described. Moreover, private landowners understandably can conclude that they are still bearing the costs of developing habitat conservation plans, candidate conservation agreements, and safe harbor agreements and what they might reveal regarding the extent of target species on their properties. Landowners shoulder the direct costs of conservation, even if the arrangements allow for more flexibility. For those holding federal land-use permits, such as ranchers whose access to federal grazing lands are essential to ranching viability, such cooperative options are far more limited.[46] When grazing permits are constrained under the ESA, allowed livestock levels and pastures are reduced, potentially threating ranching communities with economic and population decline.

Figure 6.2 lists annual ESA endangered or threatened species listings, recoveries, and extinctions from 1967 to 2024. Figure 6.3 reports cumulative data for listings, recoveries, and extinctions. It is important to note that the axes have different measures. The left axis of listings approaches 2,000, while the right axis of recoveries and extinctions approaches 100. The differences are used to illustrate patterns of listings, recoveries, and extinctions. It is not obvious from the data that the law is a success as supporters claim.

Listings, which place species under the Fish and Wildlife and NOAA regulatory regime, are the primary indicators of action under the law. By contrast, recoveries and extinctions as outcomes of listings are slim. While the Endangered Species Act calls for recovery, there is no realistic baseline for evaluation. The law does not require it, nor do the competing parties have incentives to provide one that weighs expected benefits and costs.

---

[46] See, for example, Shepherd, H. S. (2006). The future of livestock grazing and the Endangered Species Act. *Journal of Environmental Law and Litigation*, 21: 383. The political economy of federal land ownership and use regulation is found in Libecap, G. D. (1981). *Locking Up the Range: Federal Land Use Controls and Grazing*. Pacific Institute for Public Policy Research.

## 6.2 THE ENDANGERED SPECIES ACT (ESA) 147

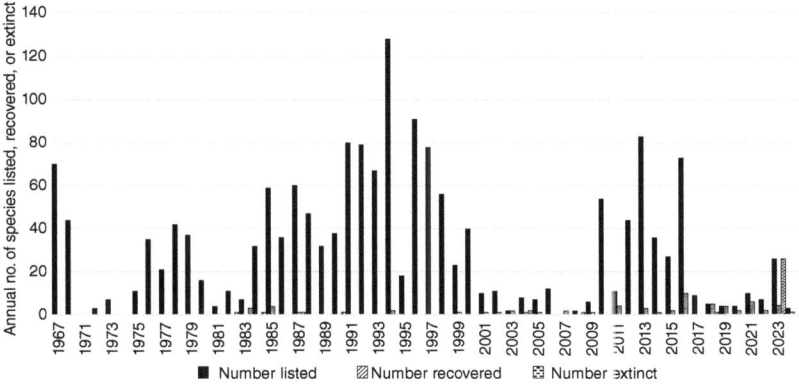

FIGURE 6.2 Annual Endangered Species Act (ESA) endangered or threatened listings, recoveries, extinctions.
*Key:* The dark vertical bars represent the annual number of species listed as threatened or endangered. The lighter shaded bars represent the annual number of species designated as extinct. The cross-hatched bars indicate the annual number of species that have recovered.
*Source:* Calculated from data in US FWS, ECOS dataset.

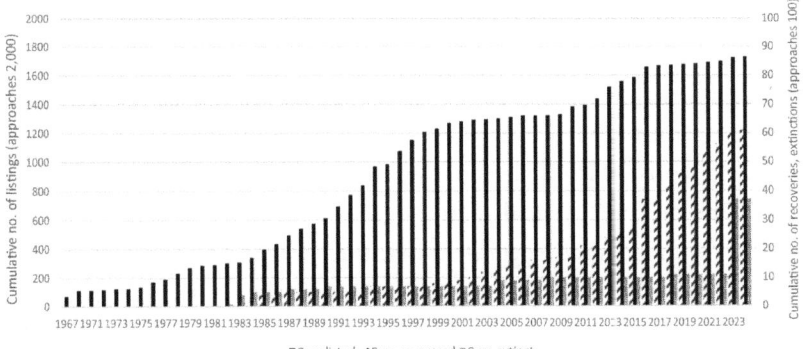

FIGURE 6.3 Cumulative Endangered Species Act (ESA) listings, recoveries, extinctions, 1967–2024.
*Key:* The dark columns represent the cumulative number of species listed as endangered or threatened as of a particular year as indicated on the left-side Y axis. The lighter columns represent the smaller cumulative number of species designated as extinct as of a set year. The cross-hatched columns represent the cumulative number of species designated as recovered as of a particular year. Both of the latter are indicated on the right-side of the Y axis.
*Source:* Calculated from data in US FWS, ECOS dataset.

Because two-thirds or more of endangered or threatened species are found on private land, the effectiveness of the ESA in achieving its recovery goals depends upon cooperation with private landowners.[47] They may be motivated to engage in preemptive harvests or other detrimental practices as mitigation.[48] Further, the law discourages information sharing about the location, number, and condition of endangered species on their properties or leased areas by landowners or federal lands permit holders. Doing so could invite the onslaught of the law and its penalties.

It is unknown just how damaging a reluctance of landholders to participate has been for ESA performance. Such positions would be very difficult to document. Even so, the recovery record seems inconsistent with the fervent support for the law and opposition to it observed in its legislative history and government and environmental NGO conclusions about it at its fiftieth anniversary December 28, 2023.[49]

Innes et al. survey private economic incentives for species preservation and show that the possibility of compensation affects habitat investments and landholders' willingness to collect and impart information about its preservation value.[50] All told, they suggest that the prescriptive nature of the Endangered Species Act could turn potential conservationists into opponents of conservation.

Preemptive critical habitat destruction or other proactive harms to endangered species to avoid ESA land-use restrictions are illegal under the law. As a result, there is little information on such

---

[47] Adler, Tarnished gold, 29–38.

[48] Ando, A. W. and Langpap, C. (2018). The economics of species conservation. *Annual Review of Resource Economics* 10: 445.

[49] See US FWS, https://shorturl.at/Kcefc; Center for Biological Diversity: www.biologicaldiversity.org/campaigns/Endangered-Species-Act-at-50/; and Defenders of Wildlife: https://defenders.org/endangered-species-act-0. In contrast, see Wright, K., and Regan, S. (2023). *Missing the Mark: How the Endangered Species Act Falls Short of Its Own Recovery Goals*. Property and Environment Research Center.

[50] Innes, R., Polasky, S., and Tschirhart, J. (1998). Takings, compensation and endangered species protection on private lands. *Journal of Economic Perspectives*, 12 (3): 35–52.

actions for systematic analysis in the literature. Two unusual illustrative examinations by Lueck and Michael and Zhang, however, reveal both private incentives and the potential negative effects on the target species.[51] The studies examine proximity of endangered red-cockaded woodpecker nesting areas in North and South Carolina on timber harvest and rotation on private lands to eliminate old-growth timber stands, needed habitat for the woodpecker.

Providing habitat for a single woodpecker colony could cost up to $200,000 in foregone timber harvests. Preemptively destroying habitat ensured landowners that the species would not inhabit their land and avoid ESA regulations that could limit or prohibit timber harvests. Lueck and Michael estimate that the observed reduction in habitat led to the potential loss of between twenty-one and sixty-seven red-cockaded woodpecker nesting colonies, close to the estimated eighty-four private land colonies already protected by the ESA. Lueck and Michael also note that a proposed North Carolina endangered species regulation to limit wetlands drainage in 1999 led to similar preemptive actions by landholders. Property owners engaged in a flurry of drainage and ditching, and annual wetlands development jumped fifteen to twenty times in a few months in anticipation of the regulation. Finally, Zhang finds that regulatory uncertainty and lack of positive incentives under the ESA make a landowner 25 percent more likely to harvest forest if red-cockaded woodpeckers nest within a mile of the property.[52]

These findings of habitat destruction illustrate the downsides for conservation when costs are disproportionately levied on some for the provision of a public good. The perverse but understandable motivations were described in 1993 by Sam Hamilton, former Director of the US Fish and Wildlife Service: "The incentives are wrong here.

---

[51] Lueck and Michael, Preemptive habitat destruction; Zhang, D. (2004). Endangered species and timber harvesting: The case of red-cockaded woodpeckers. *Economic Inquiry* 32: 150–165.

[52] Zhang, Endangered species and timber harvesting, 160.

If I have a rare metal on my property, its value goes up. But if a rare bird occupied the land, its value disappears."[53] This comment underscores the anecdotal notion of "shoot, shovel and shut up," that undermines societal efforts to protect species.[54]

The northern spotted owl controversy in the Pacific Northwest also illustrates how the Endangered Species Act has become a rallying call and cautionary tale for both advocates and critics. It also suggests how rent-seeking can raise costs and lead to inequitable administration of environmental laws. The owl's listing in 1990 led to reduced logging on designated federal forests by 80 percent. There were major reported economic losses of between 16,000 and 32,000 blue-collar jobs, between 14 and 28 percent of timber industry employment in the counties with northern spotted owl habitat, along with lower property values and out migration from lumbering communities. In the midst of ongoing conflict between rural inhabitants and environmental groups, the owl's population has continued to decline in the face of habitat loss from wildfires and the expansion of a competitor, the barred owl.[55] In July 2024, the FWS announced plans to destroy potentially hundreds of thousands of barred owls to offset the continued decline in spotted owl populations, despite the mandated halting of logging in the region that was long in place.[56]

---

[53] Quoted in Adler, J. H. (2009). The leaky ark: The failure of Endangered Species Act regulation on private land. *Case Research Paper Series in Legal Studies, Working Paper 09-34*, December. 17.

[54] See also, Thompson, B. H. Jr. (1997). The Endangered Species Act: A case study in takings and incentives. *Stanford Law Review*, 49: 305, 348.

[55] Ferris, A. E. and Frank, E. G. (2021). Labor market impacts of land protection: The Northern Spotted Owl. *Journal of Environmental Economics and Management*, 109 (C). See also US Fish and Wildlife Service, Endangered and Threatened Wildlife and Plants: 12-month finding for the Northern Spotted Owl, 85 Fed. Reg. 81144, 81152 (December 15, 2020). A Rule by the Fish and Wildlife Service on 12/15/2020. https://shorturl.at/hV4be. As the owl's population continues to decline, it has become clear that halting logging is not enough to recover the species. The forests that sustain the owl now face the growing threat of severe wildfires that destroy the owl's habitat along with the arrival of a completive species, the barred owl.

[56] https://shorturl.at/3cUd6.

## 6.3 CONCLUSION: LESSONS OF RENT-SEEKING IN THE ENDANGERED SPECIES ACT

There are several reasons for the adoption of centralized regulation rather than decentralized Coasean property rights and trade in the enactment of the Endangered Species Act. First, prescription primarily views species extinction as a biological problem to be addressed directly by identifying threat sources and eliminating them through regulatory mandates. For supporters, extinction is not an economic problem. Extinction is the biological outcome of habitat destruction and over exploitation. Economic costs and tradeoffs are not obviously relevant for proponents. Proponents pursue the certainty of government protection mandates without having to weigh costs or the potential for species recovery. They do not have to negotiate with landowners for habitat protection, which would be potentially costly and time-consuming.

Second, the attraction of policy-based rents is driven by the strongly held, normative views among advocates that evading extinction is both ethical and urgent. It is not negotiable in a Coasean sense. Avoiding extinction is viewed by supporters as so evidently desirable that costs can be viewed as inappropriate considerations. Paying landowners and government lands leaseholders to avoid harming endangered species is not considered in the legislative history. From the point of view of advocates, those who might place species at risk should cease and desist or be punished from failure to do so.

Despite the arguments of conservationists, species protection is an economic and political problem as well as a biological one, affecting the results of the ESA. In terms of economics, budget allocations and administrative personnel must be annually dedicated for conservation over long periods, perhaps very long ones. Because of the precarious situations of many species and the absence of considerations of the costs of addressing them, additional funds and staffing must be added to meet biological imperatives, even for species with little chance of recovery.

Third, rent-seeking offers policy benefits to motivated groups, who do not bear commensurate costs or as noted above, desire to have the costs made more transparent to voters. Indeed, as argued by Katrina Wyman direct compensatory payment to landholders would have made the costs of the ESA far more observable. Moreover, because costs would have had to be weighed across alternatives in that case, focus might have been more on species where recovery was feasible and not on all at-risk species as desired by conservation advocates.[57] Although general surveys indicate broad support for the ESA, they are unlikely to reveal willingness across the population to bear actual, significant costs. The surveys typically do not detail tradeoffs, costs borne by taxpayers, actions that must be taken, equity concerns, or the dire conditions of many at-risk species.[58]

The political impasse and debate surrounding the Endangered Species Act is unfortunate for the birds, animals, insects, and plants it is designed to protect; for the parties who bear direct regulatory costs; and for members of society who are concerned about them. The conflict is predictable in centralized prescriptive approaches molded by rent-seeking that do not outline negotiated conservation

---

[57] Wyman, K. M. (2008, 510). Rethinking the ESA to reflect human domination over nature. *New York University Environmental Law Journal*, 17: 490–528. Only 3 percent of species ever listed as endangered or threatened have recovered. See, Downey et al., *A Field Guide for Wildlife Recovery*. The desire of conservation advocates for broad coverage is illustrated by Michael Bean's testimony regarding 1995 ESA amendments: Statement of Michael J. Bean Chairman, Wildlife Program Environmental Defense Fund on HR 2275, The Endangered Species Conservation and Management Act of 1995, "The Practical Consequence of HR 2275 Will Be the Denial of Effective Protection for Many of Our Most Imperiled Wildlife Species." HR 2275 was to focus on species most likely to respond. Hearing Before the Committee on Resources House of Representatives One Hundred Fourth Congress First Session on H.R. 2275 A Bill to Reauthorize and Amend the Endangered Species Act of 1973 20-707CC September 20, 1995 Washington, DC Serial No. 104-37. P. 313. Representatives of the Sierra Club raised similar points.

[58] See, for example, https://shorturl.at/x6lOm. See Loomis, J. B. and White, D. S. (1996). Economic benefits of rare and endangered species: Summary and meta-analysis. *Ecological Economics* 18 (8): 197–206.

approaches and a more equal distribution of costs and benefits. Unrealistic targets are set for species that are not apt to recover, and uncompensated costs are placed on narrow segments of the population to provide ostensible, generalized benefits. Aggregate US costs are likely small, but given the tiny percentage of listed recoveries, the benefits may also be small.

# 7 What Have We Learned from the Absence of Coase?

## Implications for the Formation of Institutions

> It would clearly be desirable if the only actions performed were those in which what was gained was worth more than what was lost. But in choosing between social arrangements within the context of which individual decisions are made, we have to bear in mind that a change in the existing system which will lead to an improvement in some decisions may well lead to a worsening of others. Furthermore, we have to take into account the costs involved in operating the various social arrangements (whether it be the working of a market or of a government department), as well as the costs involved in moving to a new system. In devising and choosing between social arrangements we should have regard for the total effect. This, above all, is the change in approach which I am advocating.
>
> Coase, The problem of social cost.

### 7.1 THE SURPRISING ABSENCE OF COASE IN ENVIRONMENTAL LEGISLATION

This final chapter summarizes key arguments about how the neglect of decentralized property rights and markets as central elements of US environmental legislation can inform overall institutional formation. Although transaction cost efficiencies motivate private institutional change as described by Coase, Demsetz, Williamson, Cheung, and Barzel, they have not been not been major drivers in government policy.[1] This assessment is important for government public goods provision, efficiency, and general welfare. Policy instead is molded in many ways by rent-seeking among political actors, not altruism

---

[1] Coase, The problem of social cost; Demsetz, Toward a theory of property rights; Cheung, The structure of a contract; Barzel, Measurement cost and the organization of markets; Williamson, Transaction cost economics.

or economic proficiency. Where public goods can be provided only with government action, then caution and oversight are critical in order to limit the costs of rent-seeking. Multiple competitive interest groups can be an important source of supervision and discipline. Coase stressed that market failure arguments as justification for government intervention to address externalities may not hold upon inspection. There can be opportunities for private rights and markets, and they usefully could be considered as an alternative.

The volume examines how and why Coasean approaches are absent as principal drivers in US environmental policies. It goes beyond explanations as to the rare use of incentive instruments existing prescriptive regulation.[2] It asks why decentralized market frameworks were not adopted in the first place.

Coase sought to illustrate conceptually how property rights and dispersed exchange could provide transaction cost efficiencies in externality mitigation, and hence be more effective.[3] He suggested a policy framework, not an organizational agenda. In *The Problem of Social Cost*, he criticized standard approaches that he associated with Pigou as potentially inefficient where the solutions could be more costly than the problems. He recognized that transaction costs would affect the allocation of property rights and the extent of exchange. Coase asserted, however, that it was not obvious that transaction costs were lower in the political arena. Case by case comparisons were required to determine the transaction costs and welfare advantages of decentralized versus centralized approaches.

Surprisingly, Coase's framework for property rights and bargaining to address externalities are not the primary remedies in the US environmental policies examined here. Subsequent, narrow use of incentive-based or market approaches has occurred. The broad efficiency advantages, economic welfare gains, and collaborate externality responses suggested by Coase, however, have not been achieved.

---

[2] Keohane et al., The choice of regulatory instruments.
[3] Coase, The problem of social cost.

Although higher transaction costs with Coase might explain an efficient resort to centralized regulation, there is no evidence such comparisons were made in adopting the policies examined in this volume.

The asserted reason for the dominance of centralized controls stressed here is the aim and ability of interest groups, politicians, and agency officials to advance their self-interests through rent-seeking rather than through economic property rights and exchange. They secure private gains via desired policies or preferential, non-tradable property rights at lower cost to them than market exchange would entail. Politicians and agency officials achieve reelection and regulatory mandates and budgets. These agents may have other, less self-serving motives but their particularistic agendas appear as major factors in policy formation.

An important lesson of Coase and the empirical record of US environmental policies is that centralized political decision making, influenced by rent-seeking, can lead to the inefficient and inequitable provision of environmental public goods, even if the latter are significant. This outcome helps to explain why US environmental laws are politically controversial, despite provision of benefits, with generally no major Congressional refinements or additions since approximately 1990.

In the volume, three US environmental policies are examined: the Clean Air Act Amendments of 1970, 1977, and 1990; the Magnuson-Stevens Fishery Act of 1976; and the Endangered Species Act of 1973. The analysis draws upon legislative histories, law reviews, and relevant economics literature. Comparative empirical tests of alternative options across these three laws are not possible because centralized controls are ubiquitous, and we generally do not observe decentralized alternatives whereby property rights would be assigned and traded in both setting and administering any production or use cap. Accordingly, actual practices are compared with hypothetical Coasean alternatives. Applying a decentralized Coasean lens to existing legislation provides a metric for assessing what might be lost, if prescriptive regulation is not the low transaction cost, efficient, and equitable option. The discussion also suggests where Coase's decentralized approach might have been adopted but was not due to rent-seeking within the political arena.

## 7.2 THE LESSONS OF COASE

In his 1960 award-winning article, Coase provided a straightforward conceptual pathway to addressing externalities, an archetypal example of market failure via decentralized negotiation rather than through centralized regulatory intervention. He proposed a method of dealing with a widespread economic concern by motivating individuals to seek solutions by bestowing property rights and permitting trade. His paper set the stage for an outpouring of insightful academic work on institutional innovations that could lower transaction costs and promote more efficient economic performance across a variety of settings. Coase's heavily cited paper stimulated subsequent analyses by Demsetz, North, Williamson, Barzel, Cheung, Acemoglu, Robinson, Johnson, and others.[4]

In the academic literature, the task of curbing externalities had long been assigned to the government for a solution under the assumption that private parties and markets could not confront them (Pigou, Bator, Baumol, Samuelson).[5] Coase, Demsetz, and Cheung, however, countered that externalities were not evidence of market failure, but of incomplete property rights and markets. Providing property rights and organizing markets could be an obvious way of reducing externality costs.

With his parables of bilateral exchange between the polluter and pollutee (the farmer whose crops were destroyed by the herder's

---

[4] North, *Structure and Change in Economic History*; *Institutions, Institutional Change and Economic Performance*; Acemoglu, Why not a political Coase theorem?, 621; North et al., *Violence and Social Orders*. Acemoglu and Robinson, *Why Nations Fail*. See also, Johnson, Disease environments; Acemoglu, Institutions, technology and prosperity; and Robinson, Paths towards the Periphery.

[5] Pigou, *The Economics of Welfare*; Bator, The anatomy of market failure; Baumol, On taxation and the control of externalities; Samuelson, The pure theory of public expenditure.

grazing livestock), Coase illustrated how the distribution and trade of economic property rights to pollute or to be free of pollution could be a low cost, efficient alternative to prescriptive controls. A seemingly intractable problem could be met straight on by facilitating mutually beneficial interaction among the parties directly involved. Coase was open to the possibility that government action might still be the low transaction costs approach to the problem, especially in multilateral, transboundary contexts. Concluding so, however, required comparison of the transaction costs of his approach with standard command and control.

As indicative of the potential, we have seen that property rights and exchange were implemented for non-observable, mobile resources in the $SO_2$ national abatement market and in regional air pollution controls in southern California under RECLAIM. In these cases, the cap was preset by regulation so that the instruments were use rights within the cap. The point is that the costs of defining rights to difficult-to-bound resources were not insurmountable. Transaction costs seemingly did not hold things back when there was an interest in assigning rights and engaging in trade. Apparently, however, in the environmental policy arena, there were objectives other than efficiency among advocates.

Following Coase, there are five clear advantages of economic property rights and decentralized exchange. One is enlisting individuals' incentives to find efficient solutions to problems when they capture the resultant net gains. This setting is similar to Williamson's analysis of agent motives within firms to determine organization boundaries, hierarchies, governance structures, strategies, and contracts. A second is flexibility in responding to critical new information on costs and benefits in institutional arrangements when agents are the residual claimants to the benefits of such responses and there are tradable instruments to facilitate them. Third is balancing marginal willingness to pay with marginal willingness to accept in market exchange and hence, equating marginal costs and benefits in transactions to confront externalities. This is perhaps the most fundamental benefit of decentralized exchange. Fourth is more transparent generation and presentation of programmatic costs and benefits so that comparisons can be made among alternative responses to externalities. The fifth is avoiding the potential losses of costly rent-seeking that can occur within government programs.

This last advantage was not addressed by Coase but is illustrated in the record of US environmental policies. In this setting, rent-seeking is prevalent, raising costs, compromising potential accomplishments, creating inequities, and likely reducing the overall surplus between aggregate benefits and costs. These outcomes are relative to more optimal externality abatement where marginal social costs and benefits are equal.

Given that his objective was to outline a conceptual bargaining framework, Coase did not examine the operation of government agents, their motives, or the outcomes of their actions. North, however, delved into this issue based on his review of Western economic history, institutional change, and economic performance. North concluded: "In fact, one of the most evident lessons from history is that political systems have an inherent tendency to produce inefficient property rights which result in stagnation or decline."[6] North's inefficient property rights were those that assigned *non-tradable* rents through the political process to specific parties for partisan gains that inhibited productive economic activities, including market formation and exchange, and retarded economic growth.

The problem arises because interest groups, politicians, and agency officials can advance their private interests through rent-seeking rather than through economic property rights and exchange. They capture pecuniary and nonpecuniary rents via chosen policies or preferential assignment of property rights at comparatively lower direct costs and with more certainty than is possible with markets. These parties are not residual claimants of transaction cost efficiencies.

---

[6] North, Institutions, transaction costs, and economic growth, 422.

Indeed, they may not benefit from expanded market activities. Rather, they gain from political rent-seeking and constraints on exchange and entry. As such, their actions are intrinsically inefficient, lowering potential welfare as documented broadly by Acemoglu; Acemoglu et al., Acemoglu and Robinson, and North et al.[7]

Coase's more narrow concern from that of North and others was how to confront externalities more efficiently. His framework *predated all* major US environmental legislation after 1970, and could usefully have informed policies, had efficiency rather than rent-seeking been the objective. Even if some externalities did not lend themselves to his suggestions, some surely would have. But as we have seen, *none* of the policies employ his framework as the primary initial response. As described in this volume, the limited use of incentive instruments has occurred late and around the edges of US environmental laws.[8] Where these instruments have been adopted, the cap remains imposed by policy, not negotiated as envisioned by Coase, and the instruments typically remain weaker than a legal property right and are implemented well after policy adoption.

The Magnuson-Stevens Fishery Act Amendments eventually allowed for the assignment of narrow property rights and restricted trade some *twenty years* after the original law was passed in 1976, and after its reliance upon input and output controls failed to confront the race to fish. It seems unlikely that this delay was due to the absence of sufficient information on fish stocks. Iceland adopted individual transferable quotas in 1975 and New Zealand in 1986 as harvest rights within total allowable catches. Were information costs so much higher in individual US fisheries where such rights might have been adopted? As we have seen, even when fishery rights were implemented, the regulatory process imposed constraints on the

---

[7] Acemoglu, Why not a political Coase theorem?, 621; Acemoglu et al., Reversal of fortune; Acemoglu and Robinson, *Why Nations Fail*; North, et al., *Violence and Social Orders*. See also, Johnson, Disease environments; Acemoglu, Institutions, technology and prosperity; and Robinson, Paths towards the periphery.

[8] Keohane et al., The choice of regulatory instruments.

allocation and alienation of the instruments in order to protect fishing by targeted small-scale fishers and communities from entry by low-cost fishers from more remote US ports. This is an example of rent-seeking to limit entry of competitors.

Moreover, in instructive examples in the Clean Air Act and Endangered Species Act, cost considerations have been *prohibited* in important aspects of their administration, a distinctly unCoasean and uneconomic requirement. The question arises, why was Coase not adopted and what do we learn from this experience for the broader understanding of institutional formation and related economic outcomes that advance welfare?

As argued in the cases provided in this volume, the lack of Coasean approaches is unlikely to have been due to relative transaction costs that favor prescriptive regulation. There is no evidence that politicians considered and selected the low transaction cost way of providing what they asserted were public goods. Moreover, while environmental public goods have indeed been delivered, they likely have been provided at higher cost, less effectively, and more inequitably than was probable with a Coasean decentralized approach. Further, conclusions in some of the environmental economics literature that property rights and Coasean exchange are irrelevant and impractical are also not based on comparing transaction costs between Coasean or command and control policies.

As stressed throughout the volume, none of the legislative histories examined in this volume reveal any serious weighing of relative costs and benefits in implementing and administering specific policy choices relative to a decentralized response. If costs seemed to be too high in Congressional debates, the response in the Clean Air Act for instance was to require "technology forcing" by industry to meet the law's air quality objectives. The counterresponse of shifting focus to a lower transaction cost, more feasible mechanism did not occur. The environmental goal was too crucial for policy makers for costs to get in the way. When or if costs became politically contentious, as in the ESA's temporary halting of the Tellico Dam in

Tennessee, then cost issues received attention. In general, however, claimed benefits have been emphasized and policy has been designed to achieve them. Costs were only of concern to advocates when they could limit citizen support for adoption, and hence often were not made transparent in policies.

In the political process, proponents lobbied for preferred programs that they would not have to directly pay for. Costs would be both spread across society as well as directed to specifically regulated parties. This record is indicative of costly rent-seeking, not of transaction cost economizing through trade. Rent-seeking in the political arena has outcompeted economic property rights and market institutions in the US environmental policies, and as North and others suggest, in many general economic settings as well.

## 7.3 RENT-SEEKING IN MAJOR ENVIRONMENTAL POLICIES

When costs and benefits are not weighed carefully in the political process, there are both distributional impacts and general losses that can compromise general well-being and conflict with programmatic goals. For example, as described in Chapter 4, provisions of the Clean Air Act impose national uniform air quality standards that also prohibit significant air quality deterioration from the standards across US regions. Although that requirement might seem reasonable to some, it imposes differential costs without commensurate benefits on populations in affected parts of the country. The US is very heterogeneous in air quality, economic activities, incomes, and terrain. Uniform standards do not fit well with such conditions, and questions arise as to the nature of any resultant costs in different parts of the country as well as motives for these provisions. Uniform standards do not consider what the baseline alternative of local pollution control might have been absent the law. They do not weigh the relevant tradeoffs citizens might have been willing to make to address local pollution while maintaining or advancing economic activities, income, and employment.

The prohibition of significant deterioration in air quality across regions and related new source review of pollution from new facilities can limit economic opportunities in affected parts of the country. Rent-seeking by incumbent polluting firms, their labor unions, and political supporters in using the provisions of the Clean Air Act to reduce competitive entry elsewhere by raising competitor costs can explain these rules. They constrain competition from the migration of plants to less polluted parts of the country from more polluted original locations. Pollution might have gone down in original regions and gone up in new locations as economic activities shifted. This could have been a low-cost solution to pollution controls. All production generates some pollution and the marginal contribution of deteriorating air quality in receiving regions might have been far less than the continuation of older plants at incumbent sites. Other than pecuniary and political rent-seeking, it is difficult to explain these provisions of the Clean Air Act. Imposing exogenously determined air qualities on all communities is not obviously welfare improving overall.

Another type of rent-seeking occurs as members of environmental NGOs gain their preferred environmental values with uniform standards that they do not have to pay for. Recall as noted in Chapter 4, in opposition to marketable permit schemes under the Clean Air Act, a representative of the Natural Resources Defense Council and the National Clean Air Coalition asserted that: "The pristine air quality in the West is a global treasure."[9] The notion was that the relocation of dirty plants to those areas should not be facilitated by the ability to purchase offset permits in more polluted regions and to transfer production and emissions to the West. While this private value is understandable, it potentially imposed nonnegotiable constraints on populations living in areas with high-quality air, regardless of the economic opportunity cost. Under the Clean Air Act, the preferences of those citizens only would be considered via the political process and not through market negotiations.

[9] Nash and Revesz, Markets and geography, 591.

As argued, uniform national standards were not needed to prevent a race to the bottom, a rhetorical argument used by proponents without theory or evidence to support the claim. The standards were also not needed to address the potentially higher transaction costs of confronting interstate air pollution. The federal government might have assisted in interstate compacts to address the issue without prescriptive standards. Intrastate, not interstate, air emissions were the focus of the Clean Air Act Amendments of 1970 and 1977 and were only addressed in the 1990 Amendments through the $SO_2$ cap-and-trade system. More localized controls, involving particulates and ground-level $SO_2$, might have involved lower transaction costs had that been the objective. As noted, these are also the same reduced local pollutants that generate major benefits reported by the EPA in its positive benefit/cost analysis for the Clean Air Act.[10]

In total, the Clean Air Act's restrictions were implemented in policy design at least in part at the behest of influential parties, either for normative, engineering, health, or for more direct political and commercial reasons. The law, designed in the political process, has allowed for limited straightforward adjustment in its restrictions in light of new information on relative cost/benefit impacts within the country. A disproportionate distribution of costs and benefits across attainment and nonattainment regions arising from rent-seeking appears to have made the Clean Air Act politically divisive. The law remains controversial, and no major amendments have been approved since 1990, despite many economic and social changes in the nation over the past thirty-five years. This situation suggests that environmental economists might explore the costs and distributional effects of the Clean Air Act in more depth than they have done to this point.[11]

---

[10] https://shorturl.at/pyQyA, where the human health benefits of reducing particulates and ground level $SO_2$ are the greatest contributors to total benefits. EPA, *The Benefits and Costs of the Clean Air Act*.

[11] Aldy et al., Looking back at 50 years of the Clean Air Act.

## 7.3 RENT-SEEKING IN MAJOR ENVIRONMENTAL POLICIES 165

In fishery regulation, examined in Chapter 5, controls on inputs and outputs were implemented sixteen years after Coase and remained for another *twenty to twenty-five* years. Only after their demonstrated failure were limited property rights adopted. This late response occurred despite the obvious need for property rights much earlier to address regulated but excessive open-access fishing. These delays do not appear to have been due to high transaction and information costs under a Coasean decentralized remedy. Instead, the implementation of rights was delayed and then molded in the regulatory process to protect politically favored constituencies. These restrictions potentially have locked-in inefficiencies by design, reducing the economic value of aquatic resources in already poor communities. Also, with growing worldwide demand for fishery products, restrictions on the trade of rights to allow for consolidation and introduction of new technologies and markets, inhibit the economic vitality of the industry. The analysis here does not question the aims of the observed property rights and market controls but rather points to their long-term costs. Even biological fish stocks may be less protected than they might have been under Coasean fishery management because property rights remain incomplete, and fishery values reduced.[12] Moreover, the limited empirical evidence available indicates that these restrictions on entry have not rebounded to generate population growth or economic activity in targeted communities.[13]

In a comparable setting, had congressional policies in US agriculture limited farm consolidation and technological change in order to protect small farms and small farming communities, US agricultural productivity might have been sharply constrained. The low food prices and high exports that characterize US agriculture and its contribution to GDP might instead have had quite different patterns. The difference between agricultural policy and the treatment of

---

[12] Grainger and Costello, Capitalizing property rights insecurity.
[13] Sutherland and Edwards, The impact of property rights to fish.

fisheries is that economic property rights to land have existed in the US for over 200 years, whereas property rights to aquatic resources have not. This situation created an opportunity for wasteful rent-seeking regulations to address the race to fish and in the assignment of property rights to favored parties.

Finally, the Endangered Species Act, examined in Chapter 6, might have employed Coasean decentralized legislative and private precedents to protect at-risk species that were in existence when the law was considered in 1973. The framers of the law, however, pointedly did not do that. Rather they drafted legislation that relied upon strict habitat protection and penalties on land users for violation. Under the law, the listing of species as threatened or endangered can result in controls on land use, lost asset values, reduced economic activity, and unemployment. These losses are not fully compensated for, with important distributional impacts that affect both the motivation for collaboration with the law's conservation agenda and its potential success.

Because most endangered species are found on private lands, the punitive nature of the law with its assigned costs and restrictions does not encourage landowners' collaboration in protection. Instead, the law's incentives are counterproductive, with potential preemptive habitat destruction by landowners. Because such actions are illegal, the empirical evidence on preemption is limited. Even so, what exists indicates that private landowners can be motivated understandably to take protective actions that undermine the preservation objectives of the law.[14] Despite the law's popularity among advocates, its empirical record of success is mixed. Perhaps as few as 3 percent of listed species have recovered. The law encourages listings, even for species that may have little chance for recovery. There is no obvious benchmark for weighing progress in light of the precarious condition of many endangered species. It is clear, however, that given the distribution of costs and benefits, the law creates an adversarial

---

[14] Lueck and Michael, Preemptive habitat destruction; Zhang, Endangered species and timber harvesting.

environment for conservation. This is an unfortunate and unpromising outcome for at-risk species. The Endangered Species Act remains mired in controversy and has not been reauthorized since 1988.

## 7.4 IMPLICATIONS FOR ECONOMIC PROPERTY RIGHTS AND RENT-SEEKING IN INSTITUTIONAL FORMATION

Are there lessons for broader institutional formation from these experiences with US environmental legislation? One lesson is that rent-seeking is prevalent in the political process. It occurs in legislation that has both general and particularistic objectives. The opportunity for some agents to use politics to their private advantage, even when such actions result in more generalized costs, may be too good an opportunity to pass up. This would especially be the case if those parties were proficient in and well placed for political action. For these parties, rent-seeking outcompetes economic property rights and markets despite any attendant broad efficiency losses. Political actors do not capture transaction cost efficiencies, generating very different motives for institutional formation as compared to those who negotiate within decentralized markets. Rent-seeking provides directed gains and preferred programmatic outcomes from government action. Because there are no ready mechanisms for redeploying politically assigned assets, as is feasible with market trades, affected resources can be frozen in their appointed uses, making the economy less dynamic and responsive.

A second lesson is that institutional formation driven by rent-seeking adds costs, reduces benefits, and can have serious distributional effects. There is little motivation among advocates to balance marginal social benefits and costs. Hence, society can benefit less, relative to a more open Coasean market framework. If transaction costs were the explanation for prescription rather than decentralized methods, this conclusion would be tempered, but there is no evidence that such costs are the reason for the prevalence of command and control programs. In the case of environmental policies other than the very extensive Clean Air Act, aggregate costs with rent-seeking are likely small because of the size of the US economy and smaller share of GNP devoted to environmental issues.

If rent-seeking outcomes can occur in high profile, ostensible public goods policies, one can only imagine what could take place with more surreptitious policies, such as specialized tariff restrictions, monopoly protections, or politically motivated subsidies provided by partisan actors. These issues are explored by North, Acemoglu, North et al., and Acemoglu and Robinson. They are repeated in the 2024 Nobel lectures of Acemoglu, Johnson, and Robinson.[15] The process of beneficial institutional change through secure property rights and markets has been shown to be critical for economic performance and well-being.[16] The planet's citizens and their prospects are made worse off whenever institutional change is driven by political rent-seeking rather than by the transaction costs efficiencies of economic property rights and markets. As Coase argued, property rights of some type and decentralized exchange to address economic problems can be more effective and welfare-advancing than are centralized, imposed remedies where rent-seeking is pervasive.

---

[15] North, *Structure and Change in Economic History*; Acemoglu, Why not a political Coase theorem?; North et al., *Violence and Social Orders*; Acemoglu and Robinson, *Why Nations Fail*; Acemoglu, Institutions, technology and prosperity; Johnson, Disease environments; and Robinson, Paths towards the periphery.

[16] La Porta et al., The economic consequences of legal origins.

# Index

AB 32 program, 91–92
Acemoglu, D., 1, 8, 27
Acheson, J., 96
Acid Rain Program, 52
*Advanced Introduction to New Institutional Economics* (Ménard and Shirley), 27
air pollution
    CAA addresses, 77
    control program, 63
    cost and benefit analyses, 82
    federal regulation, 71
    health effects of, 73
    interstate, 70
    legislation, Orford existing, 74
    from Pittsburgh area factories, 66–69
    promoting local/regional, 73
    reduction, 65
air quality, 65, 67
    decentralized approach for, 65
    enhancing cost and benefit analyses, 68
    improvement, 73
    No Significant Deterioration rule, 81
    plant migration, 82
    pristine, 68, 89
    rent-seeking for, 89–90
    standard, 64
        CAA uniform ambient, 66
        EPA nonattainment counties, 65–66
        PSD of, 78
        uniform, 162–164
Allen, D. W., 14
Apollonio, S., 96
Atlantic Wreckfish fishery, 122
attainment areas. *See also* nonattainment areas
    NAAQS in, 78
    PSD, 78, 79

bargaining, Coasean, 19–20, 93, 129, 155–156
Barzel, Y., 30
Blanket rules, in ESA, 140
British Columbia fishery, 111, 112

CAA. *See* Clean Air Act (CAA)
*Cannery Row* (Steinbeck), 105
cap-and-trade system, 90–91
Carson, Rachel, 74
catch shares, 50, 116. *See also* individual transferable quotas (ITQs)
    in fisheries property rights, 108
    property rights, constituency sentiments for, 114–115
    TAC, 106
CDQs. *See* community development quotas (CDQs)
centralized pollution control, CAA and adoption, 70–77
Cheung, N. S., 57
Christy, F. T., 106, 107
citizen court suits, 75–76
Civil Rights legislation, 72
Clay, K., 86
Clean Air Act (CAA), 2, 11, 57, 161
    addresses air pollution via, 77
    Amendments of 1970, 1977, and 1990, 4
    provisions of 1963, 77–82
    and centralized pollution control adoption, 70–77
    citizen court suit for, 75–76
    on command and control regulation, 77
    costs of, 82–88
    Daniels political origins of, 74
    economics, 76–77
    elements of, 16–17
    enactment of, 72
    EPA and, 74–75
    fossil-fuel power plants, 86–87
    Greenstone, List, and Syverson effects, 86
    health benefits, 20
    improvements, 65

Clean Air Act (cont.)
    incentive-based instruments within, 90–92
    on intrastate air pollution, 93
    law reviews and professional journal articles for, 71
    lawsuits for, 75
    No Significant Deterioration rule, 60–61
    Orford's description of, 71–74
    overview, 64–70
    PSD, air quality standard, 78
    rent-seeking, evidence, 88–90
    restrictions in policy design, 164
    Shapiro and Walker analysis, 86
    on total factor productivity, 86
    transitional costs of, 85–86
    uniform air quality standards, 162–164
    uniform ambient air quality standards, 66
Clean Water Act of 1972, 58–61
Coase, Ronald, 1, 3, 9, 27, 32, 63, 127, 154
    centralized political decision making, 156
    decentralized approach, 5, 156–157. *See also* decentralized Coasean approach
    and Demsetz, 11–12
    efficiency argument, 6–7, 9–13
    efficiency remedies, 24
    in environmental legislation, absence, 154–157
    externalities, 36, 37
    firm-level analysis, economic property rights, 14–15
    lessons of, 157–162
    property rights and bargaining, 155–156
    property rights contributions, 32–39
    suggestions, 4
    transaction costs with, 155
    *vs.* rent-seeking, economic property rights and, 96–102
Coasean exchange, 127, 129. *See also* bargaining, Coasean
Coasean market approach, 19
command and control regulation, 10, 43, 53
    CAA on, 77
    rent-seeking approach to, 16–17
community development quotas (CDQs), 117
Comstock Lode, 35
congressional voting pattern, 89

contractual theory, 34
cooperative fishing quotas, 117
cost and benefit analyses, 17–18, 53
    air pollution control, 82
    CAA for Congressional Research Service, 83
    enhancing air quality, 68
    EPA performance, 64
Costello, C., 20
Currie, J., 85
Cuyahoga River, 58, 59

Daniels, B., 74
decentralized Coasean approach, 5, 17, 58, 93, 156–157
    conservation, endangered species, 128
    Endangered Species Act (ESA) of 1973, 125–139
    exchange framework, 6, 70
    flexible, 61
    rent-seeking in species preservation, 128–142
    to species conservation, 130–131
Defense Department amendment (2004), 141
Demsetz, Harold, 1, 9, 11, 32, 45
    Coase and, 11–12
    property rights, 14
    contributions, 32–39
Deryugina, T., 20
divisibility, ITQs attribute, 107
Doremus, H., 140
durability, ITQs attribute, 107
Dwyer, J. P., 63

Earth Day (1970), 74
Eberhard, E. K., 124
economic growth, 39
    economic conditions in, 40
economic property rights, 11–12, 14, 21–22. *See also* property rights
    advantages of, 158–159
    assignment and exchange, 37–38
    and Coase *vs.* rent-seeking, 96–102
    empirical record, 47–51
    extent and security, 47
    in externality mitigation, 13–16
    firm-level analysis, 14–15
    in fishery, 99
    in forming institutions, 1–22
    in institutional formation, 167–168

and markets, 23–44
  academic analyses of, 29, 30
  political rent-seeking constraints on, 120–123
  overview, 45–47
  and rent-seeking, 13–19
  road map, 20–22
  US environmental laws, 55–57
    Clean Water Act of 1972, 58–61
    institutional frameworks, externality mitigation, 57–58
    overview, 51–55
economic welfare, 38
EEZs. See exclusive economic zones (EEZs)
efficiency argument, Coase, 9–13
endangered species. See also Endangered Species Act (ESA) of 1973
  definition, 139
  environment focus on, 134
  preservation, 130
Endangered Species Act (ESA) of 1973, 4, 11, 21, 94, 139–150, 161, 166–167
  1966 and 1969 legislation, 139–150
  on 1995 reform and reauthorization, 144–145
  advocates on extinction species, 131–133
  arguments in, 125–126
  costs of listing species, 135–136
  critical habitat for species, 131, 137–138
  cumulative data, 146, 147
  decentralized Coasean approach, 126–133
  economic impacts, 138
  endangered/threatened species, 146, 147
  environmental concerns and prescriptive controls, 133–139
  environmental law in, 135
  habitat conservation plan, 145–146
  House Report on, 133–134
  key factors and objectives, 140
  listing process, 141–142
  northern spotted owl in, 150
  policy benefits of rent-seeking, 152
  policy-based rents, 151
  political situation and, 152–153
  rent-seeking in, 126, 151–153
  Section 4, 139
  Section 7, 140
  Section 9, 140
  Senate Report on, 133
  species extinction in, 151
  Tellico Dam controversy, 136
Endangered Species Conservation Act of 1969, 130
Endangered Species Preservation Act of 1966, 130
environmental economics literature, 43
environmental justice, CAA, 87, 88
environmental legislation, Coasean absence in, 154–157
environmental lobby groups, 73
environmental NGOs, 17, 18, 64, 76, 128, 129, 134, 142
environmental policy, 16, 25
  government, 52
  rent-seeking in, 162–167
environmental programs, 43, 58
  enactment, 25–26
Environmental Protection Agency (EPA), 52, 56, 60
  Clean Air Act of 1970 and, 74–75
  cost and benefit analyses performance, 64
  to cost consideration, 84–85
  environmental NGOs, 76
  NAAQS, 84
  national air pollution targets/quality standards by, 79–80
  nonattainment areas, 79
    air quality standards, 65–66
  sweeping powers to, 80
environmental regulation, rent-seeking in, 8
EPA. See Environmental Protection Agency (EPA)
ESA. See Endangered Species Act (ESA) of 1973
exclusive economic zones (EEZs), 109
exclusivity, ITQs attribute, 107
externalities, 26, 36, 37, 157
  control, 54
  market failure in, 54
  Pigouvian control, 2
  privatization, 45
  property rights to, 57
  quantities, 4
  reduction, 6
  in US environmental policies, 51
externality mitigation, 6, 7, 43
  economic property rights in, 13–16
  institutional frameworks for collaborative, 57–58
  rent-seeking in, 16–19

federal air pollution regulation, 71
federal air pollution standard, 73
*Federal Register*, 56
firm governance, 14
firm-level analysis, 14–15
Fish and Wildlife Service (FWS), 56, 137, 142, 149, 150
fisherman quota scheme, 107
fishery property rights, 49–51, 99, 100
fishing derby, 111
Ford administration, 83
fossil-fuel power plants, 86–87
fragmentation, 65
FWS. *See* Fish and Wildlife Service (FWS)

Great Depression, 72
Greenhouse Reduction Fund, 92
Greenstone, M., 85, 86

Hamilton, Sam, 149
Hannesson, R., 19, 108
Holm, Poul, 103

IFQs. *See* individual fishing quotas (IFQs)
incentive mechanisms, 2
incentive-based instruments, CAA, 90–92
individual fishing quotas (IFQs), 116, 117.
    *See also* catch shares;
    individual transferable
    quotas (ITQs)
individual transferable quotas (ITQs), 50, 96, 106, 117. *See also* catch shares
    attributes of, 107
    fishery property rights in, 117–118
    as property rights in fisheries, 108
Industrial Revolution, 40
Innes, R., 148
institutional economics literature, 29–32
institutional formation process, 26
institutional revolution, 26–28
institutional scholarship, timing of, 39–42
interest groups, 10–11
International Monetary Fund, 47
interstate air pollution, 70
ITQs. *See* individual transferable quotas (ITQs)

Johnson, S. H., 27

Keohane, N., 16
Kotchen, M., 20

Leacock, Eleanor, 34
limited cap-and-trade policies, 52
limited entry regulation, failure of, 108–112
limited licensing schemes, 110, 111
List, J. A., 86
lobby groups, 16, 17, 19
    environmental, 73
local tradeoffs, 22
Lueck, D., 149

Magnuson-Stevens Fishery Act of 1976, 4, 11, 20, 94
    Amendments, 160–161
    overfishing and, 99–102
    regional management council, 100–101
    US fisheries protection, 109
Maloney, M. T., 88
marine protected areas (MPAs), 138–139
market failure argument, 26, 43, 155
market framework, 37
market-access effect, 41, 42
Marshall, Alfred, 23, 26
McCormick, R. E., 88
Melville, Herman, 103
Ménard, Claude, 27
Merrill, T. W, 16
Michael, J., 149
*Michigan* v. *Environmental Protection Agency*, 85
*Moby Dick* (Melville), 103
Monterey sardine harvest, 104–105
MPAs. *See* marine protected areas (MPAs)
Muskie of Maine, 72

NAAQS. *See* National Ambient Air Quality Standards (NAAQS)
National Ambient Air Quality Standards (NAAQS), 69, 75, 76, 77, 81, 93
*National Audubon* v. *Superior Court*, 135
National Oceanic and Atmospheric Administration (NOAA), 56
National water quality standard, 60
National Wildlife Refuge System, 130
Nelson, Gaylord, 74
New Deal, 72
New England Council, 110
New Source Emission Review, 77, 78–79
Nixon, Richard, 124
No Significant Deterioration rule, 60–61, 81

NOAA. *See* National Oceanic and Atmospheric Administration (NOAA)
nonattainment areas
  ambient air quality standards, CAA, 66
  EPA, 65–66, 79
  New Source Emission Review, 78–79
  PSD, 78
  total factor productivity, CAA on, 86
nonpecuniary normative objectives, 53
nonpoint source pollution, 61
North, D., 23, 26, 27, 32, 42, 45, 159
  institutions definition, 32

open-access fisheries, 96, 97
  addressing, 105–108
  collective management, 98
  reaction to, 108–117
  state-imposed regulations, 97
Orford, A. D., 71–74
Ostrom, E., 27, 129
overfishing, 96–102
  economic and biological, 102–105

Pacific Northwest halibut fishery, 111
Pigou's analysis, 2
Pigouvian externality control, 2
Pittsburgh, air pollution from, 66–69
policy-based transaction cost, 52
pollutants, 87
polluter-pays principle, 10, 38
polluters/pollutees, 5, 6, 60
  bilateral exchange, 157
  command and control regulation, 10
  property rights by, 11
Prevention of Significant Air Quality Deterioration (PSD), 77, 78
  attainment areas, 78, 79
  nonattainment areas, 78
*Principles of Economics* (Marshall), 23
pristine air quality, 68, 89
private conservation efforts, 54
*The Problem of Social Cost* (Coase), 2, 155
processor fishing quotas, 117
property rights, 6, 23, 87. *See also* economic property rights
  catch shares, constituency sentiments for, 114–115
  constituency positions/political limitations, 113–117
  contributions, Demsetz and Coase, 32–39
  by Demsetz, 14
  economic, 11–12, 14, 21–22
    articles with, 28
  to endangered species, 131
  and exchange, 54
  extent and security, 48
  externalities, 57
  fisheries management, 49–51, 99, 100
  GDP per capita, 47–49
  markets requirement in, 33–34
  by polluters/pollutes, 11
  progression, 34–35
  regulatory controls and limited, 108–117
  trade, 5, 9–10
  in US fishery regulation, 117–119
Property Rights Alliance, 47
Prouty of Vermont, 81
PSD. *See* Prevention of Significant Air Quality Deterioration (PSD)
PTD. *See* Public Trust Doctrine (PTD)
Public Health Service 73
Public Trust Doctrine (PTD), 75, 134–135

quantity instrument, 20

race-to-the-bottom argument, 82
railroads, 40–41
RECLAIM. *See* Regional Clean Air Incentives Market (RECLAIM)
Regional Clean Air Incentives Market (RECLAIM), 52, 92
regional fishery management council, 5, 100–101, 109
Regulatory Impact Analysis (RIA), 80
relative costs, 20
rent-seeking, 4, 7–8, 47
  for air quality, 89–90
  auctions used in, 91–92
  command and control regulation, 16–17
  economic property rights and, 13–19
  Coase vs., 96–102
  markets, 23–44
  in environmental policy, 25, 162–167
  in environmental regulation, 8
  in ESA, 126, 151–153
  evidence of, 88–90
  in externality mitigation, 16–19
  in forming institutions, 1–22

rent-seeking (cont.)
    in institutional formation, 167–168
    political assignment, 8
    political constraints on economic
        property rights/markets, 120–123
    political/economic institutions by, 47
    predictions of, 17
    road map, 20–22
    in species preservation, 125–139
    in US environmental policies, 8
Revesz, R., 16, 65
RIA. See Regulatory Impact Analysis (RIA)
Robinson, J. A., 27
Rostow, W. W., 39
    arguments, 41–42
    economic conditions, 40
    Industrial Revolution, 40

Santa Barbara oil spill (1969), 74
Scott, A., 95
Secretary of Interior, 140
security, ITQs attribute, 107
SFA. See Sustainable Fisheries Act (SFA)
Shapiro, J. S., 63, 86
Shirley, Mary, 27
*Silent Spring* (Carson), 74
SIPs. See State Implementation Plans (SIPs)
Smith, Adam, 45
Society for Institutional and Organizational Economics, 27
Sowell, T., 63
*The Stages of Economic Growth: A Non-Communist Manifesto* (Rostow), 40
State Implementation Plans (SIPs), 84
Stavins, R., 16
Steinbeck, John, 105
Stern, A. C., 71
Sustainable Fisheries Act (SFA), 116
Syverson, C., 86

TAC. See Total Annual Allowable Catch (TAC)
Tellico Dam controversy, 136, 161
*Tennessee Valley Authority v. Hill*, 132, 136
threatened species, 139
Total Annual Allowable Catch (TAC), 106
trade property rights, 5, 9–10
transaction costs, 51–52, 70, 121, 155, 158
transferability, ITQs attribute, 107

uniform air quality standards, 162–164
*Union Electric* v. *EPA*, 84
US agriculture, congressional policies in, 165–166
US environmental laws, 55–57. See also US environmental policies
    Clean Water Act of 1972, 58–61
    fishery regulation of, 54
    institutional frameworks, externality mitigation, 57–58
    overview, 51–55
US environmental policies, 4, 7, 24. See also Clean Air Act (CAA); Endangered Species Act (ESA) of 1973; Magnuson-Stevens Fishery Act of 1976
    empirical record, 156
    examination, 155, 156
    externalities in, 51
    rent-seeking in, 8
US environmental regulation, 21, 55
US fishery policy, 2, 20
US fishery regulation, 165
    economic and biological overfishing, 102–105
    limited entry regulation, failure, 108–112
    migrating fish populations in World War II, 103
    Monterey sardine harvest, 104–105
    North Atlantic fish landings, 103, 104
    overfishing, 96–102
    political rent-seeking/constraints on economic property rights/markets, 120–123
    property rights in, 117–119
        constituency positions/political limitations, 113–117

voluntary bargaining, 130

Walker, R., 63, 85–86
*Wall Street Journal*, 75
Warming, Jens, 50
water pollution, 58, 60
    nonpoint sources, 61
*The Wealth of Nations* (Smith), 45
*Weyerhaeuser Co.* v. *U.S. Fish and Wildlife Service*, 137
*Whitman* v. *American Trucking*, 84

Williamson, O. E., 12, 23, 26, 27
  firm-level analysis, economic property rights, 14–15
willingness-to-accept, 38, 129, 158
willingness-to-pay, 38, 129, 158
Wilson, J., 96

World Economic Outlook, 47
Wyman, Katrina, 152

Young/Pombo Bill, 141, 143

Zhang, D., 149

For EU product safety concerns, contact us at Calle de José Abascal, 56–1°,
28003 Madrid, Spain or eugpsr@cambridge.org.

www.ingramcontent.com/pod-product-compliance
Ingram Content Group UK Ltd.
Pitfield, Milton Keynes, MK11 3LW, UK
UKHW020142090326
468786UK00019B/1694